Be Authentic Evermore

A ROADMAP TO UNMASKING THE GREATNESS IN YOU

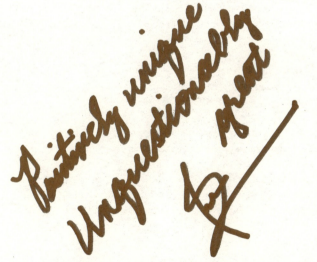

BRE JARMELL

Be Authentic Evermore

Copyright © 2016 by Bre Jarmell

All rights reserved. No part of this book may be reproduced or transmitted in any form or by any means without written permission of the author.

Moseley, A. "Philosophy of Love" Internet Encyclopedia of Philosophy. Accessed July 2016. http://www.iep.utm.edu/love/

Scripture quotations marked (NKJV) taken from the New King James Version®. Copyright © 1982 by Thomas Nelson. Used by permission. All rights reserved.

Scripture quotations marked (NIV) are taken from the Holy Bible, New International Version®, NIV®. Copyright © 1973, 1978, 1984, 2011 by Biblica, Inc.™ Used by permission of Zondervan. All rights reserved worldwide. www.zondervan.com. The "NIV" and "New International Version" are trademarks registered in the United States Patent and Trademark Office by Biblica, Inc.™

Scripture quotations marked (MSG) taken from The Message. Copyright © 1993, 1994, 1995, 1996, 2000, 2001, 2002. Used by permission of NavPress Publishing Group.

Scripture quotations marked (KJV) are taken from the Holy Bible, King James Version (Public Domain).

Scripture quotations are from the (ESV) ® Bible the Holy Bible, English Standard Version®, copyright © 2001 by Crossway, a publishing ministry of Good News Publishers. Used by permission. All rights reserved."

Scripture quotations marked (NLT) are taken from the Holy Bible, New Living Translation Version© Copyright Mark R. Norton, ed., Wheaton, Illinois : Tyndale House, 1996 Used by permission. All rights reserved.

ISBN: 978-0-9972526-3-7

Library of Congress Cataloging-in-Publication: 2016918055

Printed in the United States of America

*Authenticity must lead
if greatness in life is expected to follow.*

BRE JARMELL

This book is dedicated to great women all around the world.

Contents

Acknowledgements i
Authenticity Quiz iii
Foreword v
Introduction vii
Authenticity Reigns. xvii
Scripture References xix

1   Becoming Authentic 1
2   Becoming Authentic with God. 19
3   Becoming Authentic in Love 33
4   Becoming Authentic in Relationships 45
5   Becoming Authentic with Self 63
6   Becoming Authentic in Happiness. 73
7   Becoming Authentic Evermore 83
Authenticity Reigns Part 2 87

Authenticity Reigns Declaration 88

Acknowledgements

God, You alone sit on the throne of my heart. There are not enough words to express my love for You. You have surpassed my wildest dreams, and my heart is full of gratitude. Many thanks to my family and friends for your continued prayers and support. Thank you to my team. You guys are amazing (you know who you are). Special thanks to my LB, the *baddest* book coach and editor this side of heaven. LB you exceeded my expectations and I have nothing but gratitude.

Authenticity Quiz

Be Authentic Evermore is founded on the ARM principle. This principle simply stands for **Aligning** with God, **Relinquishing** your will and **Moving** in purpose toward a life of greatness. Self-discovery is an essential component to ARMing yourself, healing from within, changing your thoughts about life, increasing your value system, and positively impacting others. Gaining the knowledge you need to tap into your "authentic greatness" may be found within the ten questions listed on the next page. Each question is worth four points for a total of forty points. But despite where you fall on the authenticity scale, *Be Authentic Evermore* is the roadmap you need to recognize your own strength, your originality, and the beauty in being authentic.

Scoring Range:

1-strongly disagree, 2- disagree, 3 – agree, 4 – strongly agree

10-15 points – I don't know about living authentically at all
16-20 points – I have not thought much about living authentically
21-25 points – I am thinking about living authentically
26-30 points – I am on the road to living authentically
31-35 points – I am almost living authentically
36-40 points – I am living authentically

1. I listen for God's voice and follow as He leads and guides me.

2. I understand my purpose and I am taking steps toward it.

3. I read God's Word regularly and apply it to my life.

4. I have made mistakes (i.e. finances, relationships, etc.) and I understand my role in the decisions made.

5. I am satisfied and happy with my current status in life (i.e. career, job, relationships, etc.).

6. I am happy with the person I allow others to see.

7. I pray or communicate with God.

8. I understand what authenticity means and how it relates to my life.

9. I understand the benefits of change and I embrace it.

10. In life, I let go and let God.

Foreword

As the Senior Pastor of New Mercies Christian Church, I meet constantly with people who struggle with discovering their divine purpose on this earth. Because of life's experiences, many have created a persona that shields people from getting to know who they really are. The issue with this is that many struggle internally and in their relationship with God because they are not fulfilling the call of God on their lives.

I am pleased and honored to write the foreword for Bre Jarmell. *Be Authentic Evermore: A Roadmap to Unmasking the Greatness in You* is a book that will help you discover your true self in God. I have known the author for many years, and I have watched her grow in the Lord. Through the process of self-evaluation, Bre Jarmell has done the work and now presents her authentic self to the world. She has written this book sharing her story, hoping to help those who read it. She details the importance of being authentic in your relationship with God, your relationships with others, and yourself. As I read this book, I was constantly reminded of the famous quote by William Shakespeare, "To thine own self be true."

Be Authentic Evermore is a book you will not want to put down. It will inspire you to take the leap of faith allowing God to remove the masks in each area in your life. The process is not going to be easy, but Bre shows you that if you are a willing vessel, nothing is impossible with God.

Pastor Jesse Curney III
Senior Pastor
New Mercies Christian Church
Lilburn, Georgia

Introduction

The sound of Louis Armstrong can be heard in the distance, signs stating "Laissez Les Bons Temps Rouler" (let the good times roll) are seen hanging from the balconies of the unique architecturally designed buildings located throughout the infamous French Quarter. Freshly made beignets, hot and ready to eat, along with the aroma of Café Du Monde's coffee quickly grabs the attention of tourists as they stroll pass the quaint riverside café located on Decatur Street. The smiles and laughter of locals and onlookers are everywhere ... welcome to New Orleans! For the majority of my life, I lived in this great city enjoying the uniqueness of its music, hospitality, cuisine and culture. I'm a *true* Southern girl.

Fat Tuesday or Mardi Gras, as it is commonly known, is a very festive time in New Orleans. Many come from near and far to partake in the extraordinary activities that make Mardi Gras and this city so well known. Fat Tuesday is considered a local holiday where schools and many businesses close in and around the area. It's cool to have a day of celebration when anything goes and nothing matters. And it is even cooler to have such a unique place in which to celebrate. It's not uncommon to see thousands of people line the city streets awaiting carnival parades during this special time of year. The sound of "throw me something mister" echoes from the mouths of Mardi Gras observers as beautifully decorated floats roll down the street. The cheerful atmosphere makes it easy for one to slip into a world full of fun and fantasy. Mardi Gras masks and costumes of every design and color imaginable allow for freedom of expression. Kings, queens, and court jesters are just a few of the characters you'll see dancing in the streets as the unique sound of Mardi Gras music is heard throughout. The air is rich and full of food, fun and folly. No one knows who's hiding behind the masks and during this festive time of year, no one cares.

The connection between Mardi Gras and the city of New Orleans dates back centuries. For some, the unique characteristics of this southern city located along the Mississippi River are only associated with this annual event. But for others, the unique, genuine culture of New Orleans remains long after the masks and costumes are taken off and Fat Tuesday comes to an end. The character that makes this city so remarkable doesn't come and go in a day or with an event. Quite the contrary, this city is rooted in character. For three hundred sixty-five days of the year, New Orleans continues to be authentic and great. You are much like this southern city. If you think greatness has slipped through your fingers, ran out the back door, or simply escaped you, dismiss those thoughts immediately.

For the same three hundred sixty-five days, greatness dwells in you and it resides in your authenticity! The roadmap to unmasking your greatness is within the pages of *Be Authentic Evermore*. This roadmap is founded on one simple principle called ARM. When you choose to **ARM** yourself (**Align** with God, **Relinquish** your will and **Move** in purpose), your greatness becomes apparent to all just as it does in this great city.

Associations are often made between success and greatness. Success is usually attributed to things that can be confirmed by ones' achievements, and greatness is determined by the level of success achieved. Individual perspective is at the center of this thought process. You make the decision about what success means to you and the goals necessary to achieve it. Acquiring a high paying job, marrying the love of your life (remember how he first looked at you, and now he's a permanent part of your existence?), completing an educational degree, welcoming a baby into the world, or getting back into your favorite pair of jeans are a few varied examples. And for some, the success story of all success stories—becoming an entrepreneur by starting a business. Being your own boss would make anyone stick their chest out or perhaps glow with the pride of success.

For my younger readers, gaining a certain popularity status, making straight A's or B's, being selected for an activity like sports, getting the lead role in the school play or doing back flips and cartwheels well enough to make the cheering squad may be how this generation puts value on success. Many view success as accomplishing major goals, while others feel satisfied simply beginning a task and finishing it. What is obvious to me is that success is strictly an individual mindset toward a given thing. Greatness, on the other hand, is quite different. It resides in your very make-up. You are great because the Creator of the universe and all that encompasses it (that includes you) is great. The apostle Paul, composer of most of the books in the New Testament, assures us that there is "One God, the Father of all, who is over all, through all and in all" (Ephesians 4:6 NIV). Who could deny the greatness in that statement? When it comes to God, success and greatness originate from the same place—in Him. Although God has given us earthly parents to give us life, love, and to nurture us, we can confidently proclaim that the Creator, God Himself, is our Heavenly Father and there is none greater.

Has there ever been a time when you were instantly picked out as your parents' child. Maybe it was dad's deep dimples, mom's beautiful eyes, or other unquestionable characteristics or mannerisms that connect you to your parents. It is the genetic mechanism of deoxyribonucleic acid or DNA, as it is commonly known, that makes this comparison possible. This same concept holds true for God and His children. Greatness abides in you simply because you share the same DNA as your Heavenly Father. When you identify with the magnitude and power of God and align yourself with Him, it is easy to adopt the notion of your own greatness. This simple act gives you the boldness and confidence to willingly allow others to see and experience who you are from a true central place. I am guilty of living a large portion of my life out of sync with God, doing my own thing, desiring my own will, and existing well below His expectations and my level of greatness. But God is faithful; keep reading.

Time after time, God's love, grace, mercy; His friendship, His anger, and His discipline are all vividly illustrated throughout the Bible in the numerous scriptures and parables we read. Withholding nothing, God is real and genuine in His character and what He displays to us. The manifestation of these very diverse characteristics never changes who God is. He remains our loving Father. We can then conclude that authenticity directly aligns with God. When you allow Him to sit in your driver's seat, having full control while you ride through the highs and lows of life, you begin to look like Him. His presence prompts you to act in ways that are honest and true. Your playbook begins to change. The awesome state of being real and genuine takes center stage in your very being. All of the distinct character traits that make you who you are permeate outwardly for all to see. Walking with God then becomes vital to achieving your individual goals and impacting others.

Self-evaluation is a necessary step in the process of becoming authentic and tapping into your greatness. You must first become honest and real with yourself, making a conscious decision toward being the best you that you can possibly be. This involves work, work, and more work. Allowing God to grow and mature you through life's experiences takes commitment. Apart from Him, being your best you is an impossible task to take on. Intimacy with God and the ingestion of His Word (eating and absorbing it daily, allowing it to fully nourish your mind, body, and soul) opens His heart to you even wider.

Be Authentic Evermore

It creates a pathway toward a more beautiful and authentic version of yourself. This pathway may be met with bumps in the road, obstacles, and distractions. But most things we desire greatly and fully commit to have these same challenges. Give it all to God and He will make you victorious in all of it. I promise.

You must remain focused, diligent, and stay the course. You can't give up or give in. Remember, authenticity must lead if greatness in life is expected to follow. God sacrificed His son Jesus to redeem us back to Him and give us life. The formula for greatness came to earth and died on Calvary's cross for you and me. In addition, He left His Spirit and has provided everything needed to compose the ultimate instructional manual for life—the Bible. Now all you have to do is follow the formula. Literally follow God's instructions and Jesus' example and there you have it. Authenticity and success collide, and greatness springs forth.

One of the best feelings in the world is when others are impacted by my transparency. There is such a natural and free sense of wholeness in just being genuine, allowing others to really get to know who I am. There are those who see me as being very spiritual, giving great solid and sound advice. Some find me quite humorous and my conversations hilarious at times, while others see my more serious side and how meticulous I can be about things. I prefer to think of myself as having a healthy dose of everything necessary to be the best version of me that I can be. Many factors shape who we are and who we will become. Life's experiences provide significant lessons. Most of these lessons become the change agent that makes you better and propels you forward in both life and in purpose. How you view an experience often determines the degree of impact it will have in your life. Some experiences are smooth and may even be considered "walks in the park," while others may be met with difficulty, feeling more like you are trudging through quick sand. But despite the variables associated with your "easy breezy" walk or your "somebody save me" trudge, you must be willing to be transparent about the things that help shape you. God never allows you to experience life and gain from lessons that will not benefit others. God's timing coupled with your story may be what is needed to encourage someone or assist in setting them free. It's a win-win. Authenticity then becomes the bread of life for you (necessary for sustaining), and the seed of life for someone else (necessary for maturing).

We live in a world full of distractions all vying for our attention. At times, these distractions may cloud our vision. Our pursuit, passions, and desires toward purpose often take a backseat in the midst of this fog. Our efforts become sidelined by what appears to be popular in our modern-day society. At times, I have lost my footing in this sea of lies and deception. Perhaps you can relate. Simply put, we have been blindsided and taken off course by numerous untruths. We're able to find information on how we should look, act, and feel about anything with the click of a mouse. I've often had to ask myself if the information obtained says what God's Word says about me, about life, and how to navigate through it. What you accept as truth and what you allow to guide your actions is significant. God's purpose and plans for you cannot be achieved without being completely genuine in the skin you are in.

Be Authentic Evermore is an informative roadmap aimed at assisting you on the path to the greatness inside of you. Its unique and refreshing approach helps you regain your strength from life's distractions and reclaim your power by living authentically day in and day out. Throughout this book, I will share biblical truths and my own experiences that have helped me in my quest to be genuine with myself and others while I pursue my God-ordained purpose. God commissions us to "love your neighbor as yourself" (Matthew 22:39 ESV). Be it professional or personal, I welcome information shared by others. I love reading relatable, heartwarming stories that make me say, "Wow, that's me," letting me know I am not alone. Eagerness overtakes me as I gain insight that I may not have uncovered in the past. My newfound knowledge coupled with faith leaves me feeling hopeful.

As you read through this book, you may see yourself in these pages or have an "aha" moment of revelation. I may even provide you with a bit of new information. Whatever the scenario, allow my stories and God's truth to speak to you. Allow *Be Authentic Evermore* to take you on a journey of self-evaluation and discovery, helping you unmask everything blocking your success and greatness. It will whisper to your heart, prompt you to reflect, and redefine your thoughts and actions while supporting you in living a consistently purposeful and authentic life.

INTRODUCTION

Throughout this book, you will see me reference the blessed triune of God—God the Father, God the Son (Jesus), and God the Holy Spirit. All three persons share the same omniscient (knows all), omnipotent (all powerful), omnipresent (ability to be everywhere at one time) character. They are one in the same. It's my desire and prayer that you have the most life changing, joyous, and memorable experience as you read *Be Authentic Evermore*.

Authenticity Reigns

Authenticity reigns in this spot where I stand
And when you look at me you see the entire woman I am
Lies and deception running rampant in the earth
Denying you of the beauty you've been given from your birth
It's easy to buy in to what we see and hear
The enemy so subtle, you can't even see the real you disappear
Your mind, body, and soul caught up in what you think is truth
Truth so distorted you wouldn't know truth if it slapped you
But lies and deception are always brought to light
Because authenticity must reign before you can take flight
and soar becoming who you were created to be
Fulfilling your purpose and your God-ordained destiny
Authenticity moves with me like the billowing wind
So evident and a part of me it acts like my identical twin
Authenticity reigns when I utter a word
My realness, so real it's undeniably heard
I don't have time to hide my truth.
My story speaks to who I am and it may speak to you
My truth, my story, my light to be seen,
I once was lost but now I'm found
Was blind, but now I see
I wear my authenticity evermore because authenticity reigns in me

Scripture References

God Is...
- For the Lord is the great God and the great King above all gods (Psalm 95:3 NKJV).
- He won't let you stumble, your Guardian God won't fall asleep (Psalm 121:3 MSG).
- Father of orphans, champion of widows (Psalm 68:5 MSG).
- Greater love has no one than this: to lay down one's life for one's friends (John 15:13 NIV).
- God, you're my refuge. I trust in you and I'm safe (Psalm 91:2 MSG).
- If any of you lacks wisdom, you should ask God, who gives generously to all without finding fault (James 1:5 NIV).
- All praise to the God and Father of our Master, Jesus the Messiah! Father of all mercy! God of all healing counsel! He comes alongside us when we go through hard times, and before you know it, He brings us alongside someone else who is going through hard times so that

we can be there for that person just as God was there for us (2 Corinthians 1:3 MSG).

- The Lord is merciful and gracious, slow to anger and abounding in grace (Psalm 103:8 NKJV).
- Help comes from the Lord who made heaven and earth (Psalm 121:2 NKJV).

With God I Am…

- I praise you because I am fearfully and wonderfully made (Psalm 139:14 NIV).
- Charm is deceitful, and beauty is vain, but a woman who fears the LORD is to be praised (Proverbs 31:30 NKJV).
- She is more precious than rubies; nothing you desire can compare with her (Proverbs 3: 15 NIV).
- Those who look to Him are radiant; their faces are never covered with shame (Psalms 34:5 NIV).
- Blessed are those who hunger and thirst for righteousness, for they will be filled (Matthew 5:8 NIV).
- He has made everything beautiful in its time (Ecclesiastes 3:11 NIV).
- What marvelous love the Father has extended to us! Just look at it—we're called children of God (1 John 3:1 MSG).
- I can do all things through Christ that strengthens me (Philippians 4:13 NKJV).
- The Lord's unfailing love surrounds the man who trusts in Him (Psalm 32:10 NIV).

ARMing Yourself with Affirmations

- I am powerful. I am strong. I have everything I need for the day.
- I am fearless. I have God's spirit. I am a force to be reckoned with.
- I have the mind of Christ. I am God's ambassador.
- I can achieve whatever I set my mind to.
- God always wins, so I win. My purpose is needed. I can and I will.
- Hello, beautiful!
- God, I believe everything you say about me.
- God, You are my partner. I trust You.
- My steps are intentional. Every day I move with purpose.
- I have the faith I need to climb this mountain.
- I see myself at the top. Hello, world!
- There's greatness in me.

CHAPTER ONE

Becoming Authentic

There is something so wonderful about living an authentic lifestyle. When you embrace who you are and freely allow others to see and know the real you, you offer gratitude and praise to God in a way that can be witnessed by many. Leonardo da Vinci and Michelangelo have been hailed as two of the world's greatest artists. Their artistic skills have been depicted in paintings such as The Mona Lisa, The Last Supper, and The Creation of Adam. The level of thought and creativity observed in these works of art suggests both artists exercised a degree of authority and power in the skills they possessed. Their work has impacted many lives, causing others to bravely attempt duplication of these masterful art pieces. But they are unique. There can only be one original—such is the authority and power that encompasses our omniscient God.

God also exercised His thought and creativity by designing a unique and original version of you. And He has placed everything in you needed to demonstrate your uniqueness and originality to the world. You just need to step into it. In the beginning, God looked over everything He had made—it was so good, so very good (Genesis 1:31 MSG). If God looks at you with satisfaction and pleasure, if He values what He has created in you, then what makes us look at ourselves and act in ways that deny His divine wisdom? What makes us behave in ways that lack our genuine nature?

... there is no amount of money, nor are there any connections or affiliations, and no degree of smarts that can take you where authenticity can.

Authenticity is like a magnet. It is pure attraction. Nothing needs to be added or subtracted to draw you to it. It attracts you to persons, places, and things that in some form or fashion help you in being and becoming a better you. Oftentimes, the way we think and behave is learned. But authenticity is all about who you are and what you exhibit from your core (that central place of existing). It is that inward place that knows nothing but what is true about you. The purity you possess is birthed out of the natural characteristics and qualities that make you unique. Your genuineness is embodied in that same pureness, uniqueness, and originality.

We choose what we allow people to see and know about us. When you grant others an opportunity to see who you are from a true and inward place, you display the awesome artistry of God. Throughout your display you make reference of His omniscience by embracing and loving the person He has so skillfully created from the inside out. This allows the authentic nature of God to be evident in your daily life. The power dwelling on the inside of you is ignited, unlocking your inner beast. This small act is a good indication of the degree of trust you have in your Heavenly Father.

One of my favorite books of the Bible is the book of Proverbs. It has been termed the book of wisdom and virtue. Proverbs shows you chapter by chapter and verse by verse how to wisely navigate through life. One of my favorite scriptures from this book affirms my trust in God and His plans for me. That scripture is "Trust in the Lord with all your heart and lean not unto your own understanding; in all your ways submit to Him and He will make your paths straight" (Proverbs 3:5-6 NIV). Now this is good news to me. With all of the crooked paths I have taken in life, it would be sheer insanity for me not to fully submit to God and trust in His guidance. But if I am going to be real with you, I must admit that even in knowing and oftentimes quoting this very scripture, I still have not always allowed God to take the lead. In addition, there have been occasions when His DNA has not been very evident in my behavior either. But despite my shortcomings, God and time are allowing the words of Proverbs 3:5-6 to be more prevalent in my life and more reliable than my own knowledge, will, or skills. He has allowed me to ARM myself for the journey ahead. Lessons gained have helped me realize that there is no amount of money, nor are there any connections or affiliations, and no degree of smarts that can take you where authenticity can. It gives you outlandish courage and boldness. Your potential for greatness is unlocked and your territory enlarged far beyond what your eyes can see or your mind can imagine. Go ahead, grab hold of this, and watch how you begin to transform and reshape your life.

The Gospel of John has been approached differently from the other three gospels in the way it begins declaring, "In the beginning was the Word and the Word was with God, and the Word was God" (John 1:1 NKJV). To add to this declaration, the writer of Proverbs proclaims "every word of God is pure" (Proverbs 30:5 NKJV). You can search the world over and over and over again and not find a more pure person than God Himself. The pureness of authenticity is centered in God (you'll hear this statement repeated throughout this book). He is the ultimate example of authenticity. Everything begins with Him. Genesis gives an account of God's thoughts toward man as He skillfully created him. "God created man in His own image; in the image of God He created him; male and female He created them" (Genesis 1:27 NKJV). He formed you from dust and blew His breath, the breath of life into you, filling you with His character. He is counting on you to walk in a God kind of authority and power just as He has done and continues to do. He has provided you with the perfect blueprint that if followed, allows you to be great in life and have an indisputable impact on the world. God wants to leave His imprint in the earth by guiding you in living authentically.

Be Authentic Evermore is birthed out of the knowledge of who God is. This magnetic behavior also develops when you are unquestionably satisfied with who you are. What arises out of this satisfaction is a willingness to let others within your inner space. Your security in God and yourself transcends any suspicions or doubts about others. This releases you to operate in a freedom that is normal and natural. But this cannot be obtained without walking daily with God. You must allow His guidance and wisdom to propel you to higher heights and keep you safe from all harm. To sum it up, being authentic evermore is how you live and demonstrate who you are daily, consistently and continuously, never changing or deviating from the unique and original masterpiece God created in you. It's as simple as ARMing yourself.

My authentic existence has become paramount for me. Here's something to think about. Did you know when you operate in ways that are void of your uniqueness and originality, you delay and in some cases forfeit the very thing God created you and only you to do in the earth? I've known since I was a teenager that God had called me to do something special for the sake of the gospel. Of course it was not that I was highly experienced in hearing the voice of God during my teenage years, but there was an unshakeable feeling of love that was present when I spoke of Him. Do you remember your first kiss or the first time you uttered the words "I love you" to someone? Can you recall that warm, magical feeling that came over you every time your mind took you back to that moment? In my conversations about God, it was this sort of undeniable warmth and a unique lovefest going on between me and Him that remained present with me for years. It was like I could feel the glow of Him smiling on me. During these times, I knew I brought Him pleasure and although I did not recognize it at the time, He was doing the same for me.

My very first insightful word or prediction regarding my future life and who I would become in God came from my seventh grade teacher, Sister O. There was a fondness she and I had toward each other, more than what is expected from a student and her teacher. Sister O was super cool. She was my teacher and my friend. I was certain Sister O cared deeply about my well-being and my success in life. I admired her commitment to God, and I trusted her ability to hear from Him. One day out of the blue, I remember her telling me I was destined to do something great for God. I didn't really understand what she meant at the time but because her statement included God and I in the same sentence, I figured it had to be something good for me. However, I was a typical teenager more interested in hanging out with my friends and talking about boys than the insightful word that was spoken over my life. Little did I know, a seed had been planted in me, and it would later take root and grow. I was fifteen years old—much too young and immature to realize how profound Sister O's words were at the time.

Throughout my teenage and early adult years, God continued to pursue me, cultivating the seed that had been planted earlier. He was graciously tugging at my spirit to be an instrumental part of His divine plan in mankind's journey to salvation (accepting Jesus as Lord and Savior). After years of ducking and hiding from God and ignoring His gentle pull, I eventually gave in. I later became a seed planter for others as Sister O had been to me. Let me pause here to clarify my statement regarding God's tug on my spirit and heart. God, full of all power and glory, did not need me to assist in His divine plan for mankind to recognize their need for salvation. He is sovereign (supreme in power and authority) and Jesus had already paid the price for mankind's salvation on the cross. But God, the incomparable artist that He is, lovingly desired to use me. "So neither he who plants nor he who waters is anything, but only God who gives the growth" (1 Corinthians 3:7 ESV).

Despite my soft spoken voice, I have always had a very bold posture about God. I have never been ashamed of my belief in Him. Although I was a baby Christian at the time the seed was initially planted, there were fundamental biblical principles that I had been taught and always believed to be true. These biblical principles would become the foundational building blocks for me to grow and develop in my faith. When real-life situations and poor decisions gave rise to a lack of authenticity in my attitude and behavior, it would be a rock solid foundation that would keep me from completely losing my way.

Despite Peter's shortcomings, Jesus was confident that Peter would fulfill His predetermined plan for his life.

As years passed, I became an adult maturing and growing in God. I would be faced with many challenges and situations—the biggest including health issues, finances, and let me not forget the relationship blunders. But my first lines of defense in times of trouble were prayer, God and His Word, prayer, and did I say prayer? Perhaps through these challenges and my responses to them, God was allowing me to actively participate in my own cultivation process. While attending New Mercies Christian Church (NMCC), a local church located outside of Atlanta, Georgia, I became a member of the evangelism ministry (sharing the gospel of Jesus with others). Our mission was to invade the enemy's camp and minister Jesus to anyone who would listen. I was eager and excited to fulfill this mission and with every bit of boldness in me, I knocked on stranger's doors and unequivocally asked, "Do you know Jesus? Is He your savior?" I stood courageously proclaiming Him, His love, and His goodness to people who sometimes looked at me like I had ten heads. As bold as I was, I felt unmoved by these expressions. I knew I had to plant the seed of truth that would one day grow and be life changing for those I encountered.

The evangelism ministry was a nice holding spot for me. I was doing just enough to think that I was fully operating in all God planned for me to do in this life. But my complacency and delusion would soon become evident. You remember the disciple Peter? He was passionate, bold in character, firm in his faith and love for his master, Jesus—the Jesus he left everything to follow. You may also remember Peter as the disciple who firmly denied any affiliation with Jesus not once, but three times on the night Jesus was betrayed. Peter's unwavering faith and immense love for Jesus had been tested just as real-life situations and experiences test our resolve and love for God's blessed triune.

An artist has the natural ability to pick out flaws in their work when others fail to detect imperfections at all. With these hidden imperfections, these skilled craftsmen remain proud of the art they have created and continue to make use of it, allowing others to be warmly impacted by it. Jesus, in His omniscience, knew that at a crucial moment in history, Peter would not only deny his faith but deny Him, the one person who Peter had grown to love and trust immensely. But He was also aware of the invaluable assets that had been deposited in Peter and of the purpose that had been planned for him. Despite Peter's shortcomings, Jesus was confident that Peter would fulfill His predetermined plan for his life. Peter went on to become one of the most revered and talked about followers of Jesus Christ.

So, did I really believe that the modern-day bold, passionate clone of the disciple Peter (as I was often referred to by my evangelism pastor) had tapped into all that God had planned for her to do? I did. Could it really be that easy? I thought it was. But the tug on my heart that I spoke of earlier remained. I was only fooling myself. These superficial thoughts had me outwardly living in a state of disillusion. Deep within my heart I knew God had more for me to do. Many days were spent thinking about what laid ahead for me. I was comfortable knocking on doors and leading others to Christ, but to submit to anything else from God would require allowing Him to stretch me in ways I was not prepared for. In hindsight, I realize that although I was indeed impacting God's kingdom, I had not embraced my uniqueness and originality to its greatest potential. I had not submitted to God's full plan for me. Through years of pain and emptiness, chasing my own hopes and dreams, I finally recognized that I was very dissatisfied with my life and the direction in which it was going.

In 2005, I thought I had grown tall enough spiritually. I was ready to put on my "anointed woman of God" shoes. I felt ready to accept whatever else God had planned for me. Here's a bit of good news for you. God's thoughts are not our thoughts. He always thinks more about you than you could possibly think about yourself. This is probably because He knows you best. God is well aware of all He has deposited in you. So after a great deal of prayer, I made the decision to launch out into the deep. In 2005, I became a minister-in-training at New Mercies Christian Church. Wow! You didn't see that coming did you? Neither did I at the time, but I was sure this was the path God was leading me on.

January 15, 2006 was a glorious day. After a year of studies and testing, I was ordained and licensed as a minister of the gospel. Here's where I dance and shout, "Glory to God!" I shouted that day, but the exuberant emotion slipped away from me quickly. What was funny—well, perhaps not so funny but true (I am supposed to be authentic, right?) was I did not want anyone besides the New Mercies family to know about my new position in God. Although I loved God and in my heart felt appointed for this task by Him, wearing the title of a minister was overwhelming and sadly unappealing to me. And it surely was not a fashion statement for me to wear a long black robe and a white collar around my neck. So, I guess you are wondering (as I did), what happened to submitting to God and being serious about His plans? Where had the "anointed woman of God" run to? My boldness, confidence, and commitment in who I was obviously had its limits. I was comfortable leading people to Christ in a one-on-one setting. But I was so very uncomfortable with many of the other requirements entailed in embracing this special call on my life.

Fear will choke purpose and destiny right out of you eventually leaving you empty if you let it.

Training continued after the licensure and there were specific expectations outlined. Continued education was a requirement. Leading congregational prayer and possibly going before the congregation to preach were also requirements. For many that know me personally and know my heart, these tasks seemed perfect for me. But here's where I act like the star of the hit movie *Forrest Gump*—Run, Minister! Run! I shuttered at the mere thought of standing in front of a congregation—all eyes on me. My mind often trying to bargain with God thinking, *God, I'll do anything, but this is the deal breaker.* I always believed it was the anointed sermons that moved people to tears, made their feet dance, and caused them to act as if they were truly free. Did I have the ability to touch people in ways that would free them at their most vulnerable point? I felt like Moses who was afraid and resistant to his call to leadership over the children of Israel because he stuttered. My quivering, soft spoken voice coupled with a pair of shaky knees is the paralyzing thought and image that would not escape me. What on earth could I have been thinking by doing this?

I desired to please God, I sincerely did. I wanted what He was offering to me just on my terms. In my heart, I was no closer to purpose than when I started the ministers-in-training curriculum. After all the time and effort spent studying God's Word and learning how to authentically lead others, my actions remained disingenuous. Fear had stifled me. Here's a nugget of truth for you. Fear will choke purpose and destiny right out of you eventually leaving you empty if you let it. But all of the fear that was meant for my demise, God was using for my good. It would all be part of my process toward spiritual growth, development, and a heart that is true and genuine.

I have intentionally taken you on my spiritual journey toward authenticity so you may fully understand how it relates to my purpose and greatness in life. But I would be remiss if I did not unveil a few other points. I recall numerous occasions when I have quoted scripture, crying out to God in times of need. Those foundational principles and scriptures planted from my youth served as my strength during those instances. But just as Peter fell short in denying His Savior, so have I. Denying God and His Word to have full authority over me is a form of rejection that I must admit.

Here are a few examples of what I mean. What about withholding my tithes so I could buy another pair of shoes I did not need, failing to spend time with God in prayer, or missing Wednesday night Bible study just so I could watch the broken lives of others on TV? My flesh often served as commander-in-chief over my life instead of God Himself, putting my spirit and God's plan for me in jeopardy. The Apostle Paul reminds us, "For I know that nothing good dwells in me, that is, in my flesh; for the willing is present in me, but the doing of the good is not" (Romans 7:18 NASV). God, loving Father, relentless in His pursuit of me gave me time to grow and develop through my process. More years, more time, and more growth would be in my future. I remain in training camp constantly evolving, becoming more obedient, submissive, and completely satisfied with my uniqueness and originality. With God's patience, love and grace, I have ARMed myself.

I have indeed become authentic. In *Be Authentic Evermore*, everything you have read and shall read is living proof of God's unparalleled ability to do in you what nothing and no one else can.

On June 21, 2013, 8:20 a.m., my world as I knew it changed. I was diagnosed with breast cancer. After receiving such a serious diagnosis, every pertinent matter in my life (spirit, health, and wealth) gained priority status. Success as I knew it was crucial. I did not think I was suddenly doomed to death because cancer had secretly and quietly crept in and decided to take up residence in my body. But as a nurse, I knew the severity of this kind of diagnosis, and it scared me. I was reassured about the varied treatment options for cancer and the positive lasting results that these options bring. But this was a crucial time; I needed to dig deep.

My recollection of the biblical story of Lazarus being raised from the dead, the woman healed after battling a blood disorder for years, the lame that walked, and the mute that talked became more reassuring to me. My faith and trust in God coupled with a strong belief that He had destined me for something big aided me in enduring this unwanted battle with the enemy. Romans 8:28 (NKJV) reminds me in whom I should trust, "And we know that all things work together for good to those who love God, to those who are the called according to His purpose." I love Benjamin Franklin's quote "Don't put off tomorrow what you can do today." During this time, this quote helped me put things in perspective and remain laser focused on the road ahead.

...Beloved, don't be afraid, trust in Me.

The gorgeous shoes and the stunning outfit placed on my must-have list just days prior to my diagnosis seemed to lose their appeal. It was more important for me to gain financial stability. I took the battle of the bulge to level one thousand. Those stubborn ten pounds that made themselves at home had to go. There would be no more chocolate cake for me, crushing to say the least (you'll understand why as you read on). And that last bit of good sleep that met me every morning during the 6:30 a.m. hour would be replaced with a daily six to eight mile walk/run.

Happiness could no longer escape me today in hopes of finding it tomorrow. Living life to its fullest and maintaining an orderly regimen was my pressing reality. But what was even more pressing and paramount for me was purpose. This time my pursuit would be real. God in His sovereignty allowed this tumultuous event to occur in my life, but He carried me through the storm with a plan for my good. In a very strange way, cancer saved my life. It would become the game changer. Indeed, I became purpose-driven. For the first time in my life, I would fully submit and commit to God's plan. The evidence of you holding this book in your hand is proof of my commitment.

During this time, I began to pray more fervently, pressing God about everything He had breathed into me. I declared that I never wanted to be in a position where I felt I could possibly leave this earth and not have poured out every drop of everything God had placed in me. I wanted nothing left in my tank. When the time would come for me to meet my Savior, I wanted my fuel light to say EMPTIED OUT. Days passed, and I continued to press God about my future. His answer to me was not immediate but right on time. One special night after an intense moment of intimacy with Him, He birthed my first poetic piece entitled *TIME*. Who says God doesn't have a sense of humor? God in all of His glorious wit granted me a poetic piece that speaks to His faithfulness and love as time, meaningful time slips by us.

Perhaps after running and hiding from my own purpose for so long, God figured I could probably tell a pretty good story regarding this subject. *TIME* speaks to the love God displays as we either embrace or run from His plans for us. What I have learned through my process is that God is more patient than most. The emotions that arise when God's truth about you and your truth about you finally meet are pretty intense. But it's a great moment, a memorable moment. Here is an excerpt from *TIME*.

<blockquote align="center">
You've given me your glory, I feel your presence
You've given me time
Time … tick tock, time and more time
You've given me your heart
I feel you, I feel your love … I feel the slipping away of time
Getting wet, my shirt is drenched. Got to get in out of the rain
</blockquote>

> Oh wow, it's just my tears
> Because you've given me time

After writing *TIME*, God poured poetic pieces into me like falling rain (no pun intended). He instructed me to compile a book about my life experiences and lessons gained that would encourage and inspire the masses. I took pen to paper writing my first book, *Melodeez of the Heart*. His confidence in me oftentimes seemed overwhelming as I listened intently to Him. I began to grasp at my future with haste and continued to pray for clarity and direction. God was requiring me to share, be genuine, transparent, and embrace a divine assignment that only I could fulfill. My unwavering transparency gave rise to personal discovery.

My writing opened the door to memorable moments of joy and happiness, some painful and shameful memories, disappointments, and face to face encounters with all of my issues. If I were going to step into purpose and destiny, I needed to confront everything that was holding me captive, keeping me from it. God further explained that I was to share the good, bad, and ugly pieces of my life—stories that are relatable, timely, and relevant to women and men. I remember thinking sharing the good is easy and later asking God, "Do you really want me to share the bad and the ugly?" I felt like a caterpillar going through its gruesome transformative process to becoming a beautiful butterfly. This was painful, but I knew if I stayed the course, God would loose the chains of bondage that had held me captive for so long. Walking into my greatness would

BE AUTHENTIC EVERMORE

become my daily quest. Empty days no longer had a place in my life. I would finally be free. Here is an excerpt from *My Metamorphosis*:

> You took me by the hand
> My heart and mind You would lead
> You whispered, "Beloved, don't be afraid, trust in Me."
> Your Word washing me,
> As Your Spirit paves the way for
> Change, wonderful change

After recalling God's instructions to encourage and inspire, I decided to call my melodic poetry *inspirational clips*. These words of inspiration speak my truth—all of it. I am no longer hiding. I am authentic. My willingness to allow others into the pages of my life is the catalyst for me to continue to live out my God-ordained purpose and help others to find and live out theirs.

CHAPTER TWO

Becoming Authentic with God

Isn't it great that God not only desires but insists that we come to Him as we are? God is the only person I know that never expects me to be anything other than who I am. If I am dirty, unclean, and full of mess, God expects me to come to Him dirty, unclean, and with all of my mess. And we all have mess. It's His and only His uncanny ability to perfectly transform all of our many imperfections, making them useful for our journey and the journey of others. Isaiah 1:18 assures us "Though your sins are like scarlet, they shall be white as snow." Here again is good news. I don't proclaim to know everything, but the last time I checked, the color red and the color white lay on opposite ends of the color spectrum. Only God through His unconditional love and His amazing grace could possibly pull off this depth of transformation.

It is God's love for us that draws us to Him and to a life of authenticity.

Grasping the enormity of God can be overwhelming because He is such an awesome wonder. The very thought of Him and His miraculous works can be downright intimidating. Some may feel that the majestic nature of God and the splendor of His presence is only worthy of someone who is without faults or flaws. Nothing could be farther from the truth. It is God's love for us that draws us to Him and to a life of authenticity. Being authentic with God requires complete transparency. It's not like the very One who created you can't peek inside and see ALL that you think you are hiding from Him. But He wants you to trust Him enough to freely share the deepest, most inner parts of your existence. His desire is for you to willfully reveal to Him all that concerns you, even those areas that you may be frightfully ashamed of. But I will be the first to admit that this is not always easy to do. Guilt and shame will often make you run for cover, hiding you from the very One who has the desire and power to forgive and set you free.

Growing up in the church and learning about God and His Word, provided me with a level of spiritual stability that time has allowed me to build upon. Although I cannot add reciting the Bible from cover to cover to my list of accomplishments, I can definitively say that the Bible is full of biblical principles that, if followed, will add tremendous value to your life. There is one biblical principle in particular that stood out to me as I was writing this book. It's funny how the things that become strongholds for us remain in the forefront of our thoughts. Reminders can be good on occasion. Perhaps every now and then we need to recollect on where we have been, God's faithfulness in rescuing us from the deep, and His commitment to where we are going. The principle I am referencing speaks to fornication which is sexual engagement outside of the covenant of marriage.

As I wrote this portion of the book, I believe God pressed this topic upon my heart because fornication has become such an accepted practice within our culture. Many ignore the implications and the negative impact that fornication has on the mind, body, and spirit. We have been tricked into believing that this momentary exchange and exhalation satisfies our sense of touch and need for affection. But this is a lie. Fornication severs, separates, and destroys the beauty of love and an exchange with God that truly satisfies all things and is everlasting.

But this time it would take a little more than the settling of spring and beautiful blue skies to compare to the peace and serenity I had come to experience with God.

During my developmental years as a Christian, this subject matter was mentioned in depth and on numerous occasions in my small traditional Baptist church. Many times I wanted to crawl under the pew as pastor preached a sermon that appeared to be just for me. I wondered if God had secretly given the man of God insight of my sinful choices and was sending me a word of warning. 1 Corinthians 7: 8-9 (ESV) is clear, "To the unmarried and the widows I say that it is good for them to remain single as I am, but if they cannot exercise self-control, they should marry. For it is better to marry than to burn with passion." Throughout my adult years, I will admit I have lacked self-control in some instances. I have also lacked the desire and will to not engage in passion when offered. I failed to grasp and fully understand the consequences of such behavior. I am now enlightened by the truth that anything contrary to God's Word is dangerous and destructive. Fornication seemed then and now like part of the formula for successful dating. The devil is a liar; it is not. Here is an excerpt from *The Covenant*:

> We think it's just a blending of flesh,
> Like peanut butter and jam we come together and make something good
> But it's really a give and take of the spirit and what lays deep within
> And outside of the covenant of marriage, it's just plain ole sin

As a young adult, I seized every opportunity to develop an authentic relationship with God. I prayed regularly and consistently throughout my day. I became an avid student of the Word. I attended Bible study weekly. I even went to church twice on Sunday because honestly, I could not get enough of Him. As I spent time with Him on a regular basis, I realized how cool God was and that He has a tremendous sense of humor. Although His love and grace have always been constant, it was during this special time in my life that His love and grace appeared more evident. My relationship with Him soared to heights I had never known. I was content with just Him and me and the vibe we had going on. It was like watching two people in love behaving like they are the only people in the world. I shared everything with Him, just as He desires we do. I longed for Him and when I entered His presence, I stayed there for hours basking in the majestic aroma of all that He is.

I was young, single, and had little responsibility other than work, so it was not only easy but enjoyable to hang out with God. Soon my ability to exercise the Word I was standing on, and the intimacy and relationship I had so proudly developed with Him would be tested. In time, the writings of the Epistle of James would have significant meaning for me. "But be doers of the Word and not hearers only, deceiving yourself. For if anyone is a hearer of the word and not a doer, he is like a man observing his natural face in a mirror; for he observes himself, goes away, and immediately forgets what kind of man he was" (James 1: 22-24 NKJV).

Spring was in the air and this time around was no different than any other time when spring had arrived. The seasonal change began to awaken me to love as it always did. All of nature would sing God's praises as birds chirped and the flowers displayed an array of beautiful colors. Daffodils, tulips, and other springtime flowers popped up everywhere. I always think of this season as allowing something new to come forth. Longer days mean more opportunities. And clear blue skies create a feeling of peace and serenity. But this time it would take a little more than the settling of spring and beautiful blue skies to compare to the peace and serenity I had come to experience with God. He had become everything to me. He was not just my Father. He had become my lover and my best friend. I would awaken to Him in the mornings and fell asleep in His arms every night. I was confident, and it was evident—God alone sat on the throne of my heart. Then I met a man. For storytelling purposes, let's call him Mr. Man. He was tall, dark, sexy, and very handsome. His strength was evident and impressive to me. Here is an excerpt from *Sexy*:

> I must admit. I've heard tall, dark,
> and handsome used to describe
> this attribute that most times lays dormant on the inside.
> Is it really sexy if all that physique lacks God Himself,
> and your inner man is starving, lying dusty on a shelf?
> If your walk and your talk suggests a life that's been hard
> instead of a life that has come through
> hard times by the grace of God
> If all you can think about is yourself,
> because your sexy mind can't think about nobody else
> I guess sexiness is relative; people see what they see.

Mr. Man and I shared the same spiritual belief, and we both verbally expressed desires to please God. Our actions later would suggest something quite different. He desired to settle down and so did I, so we entered into a relationship. We talked a lot and began to get to know each other, or so I thought. So smitten, I didn't recognize the trap that was being set. For the first three months, everything was blissful. It wasn't long before we both felt like we had been bitten by the lovebug. He proposed and we celebrated together (you know what I mean). What started out as an "Oops, we made a mistake," quickly became a constant struggle with fornication again. Suddenly, my ability to be transparent with God was overshadowed by guilt and shame, and I was failing the test. (Remember I said earlier that guilt and shame will make you hide from God.) It did. Meeting God face to face in our secret place was difficult to attain partly because I began living with Mr. Man. I opened the door wide, rolled out the red carpet, and welcomed the enemy in.

Living together meant I shared an enormous amount of time and space with him and yes, we shared the same bed. I allowed him to not only reign as king of my castle but to sit on the throne of my heart. I fell asleep with him at night and it was his face that I awakened to in the mornings. Outwardly, I appeared happily satisfied, but my spirit man was dying on the inside. Once you have experienced intimacy with God and allowed Him to be the lover of your soul, no one else will suffice, and no one can fill His shoes or take His place. My fleshly desires, okay, let me be authentic and call it what it was—my sin had caused separation between God and me. Prior to Mr. Man, entering the presence of God had been smooth and void of obstacles for me. Finding and feeling God took no effort because He lived with me every second of every day. He was Father, friend, confidant, husband, and so much more. But I began to cheat on Him. Mr. Man arrived on the scene, and I seemed to have lost God. Where had my best friend gone? Why was He no longer there? Here is an excerpt from *More of You*:

> More of You is what I need I say
> Every second, every minute, every hour of each day
> You feel so distant, Your face so far away
> It's not You that has moved but in my sin, my heart
> that has strayed

Day after day and night after night, I could not find the words to pray. And fear of God's disappointment in me kept me from attending church. My struggles and inability to be transparent before God became the ball and chain that held me in bondage and separated me from Him. Sin had severed my heart, separated me from my one true love, and was destroying my spirit.

Sometimes we become complacent with people and situations that were never meant to be a part of our existence. After a few months of bliss with Mr. Man, the relationship began to take a downward turn. Hindsight really is 20/20. You know we often put on masks hiding our true selves and inner feelings. I try to be conscious of my expressions because

I have big eyes, and I have been told my eyes speak. When I am happy, they dance. And well, when I am sad, the sadness in them is what you see. Sometimes your best efforts and even the mask you put on can't hide what's really going on inside. Luke 6:45 (NIV) reminds us "For the mouth speaks what the heart is full of" and in my case, so did my eyes. Every morning during this relationship, I put on my mask that read "happily in love" and headed to work. My daily routine allowed me to grab a cup of coffee and have small chat sessions with two of the housekeepers on our floor. One morning in particular stood out to me.

I recall it as if it were yesterday. My morning buddies and I had shared a few minutes of conversation reminiscing about the happenings of the prior weekend. Time passed and as I looked up at the clock, I would only have five minutes to spare before I needed to be in position to receive report from the night shift nurse. So, I bid my coffee buddies farewell and wishes for a good day. As I walked away from them, only a few feet, I could hear one say to the other, "Her eyes are always so sad." What did she mean? Didn't my mask read happily in love? Couldn't they see that I was? Oh God, had I been exposed? My shame was no longer a hidden secret. I was wearing it. After numerous pitfalls and undeniable pain within the relationship, I began to cry out to the only person I knew could save me. My heart was breaking day after day and night after night. I'd watch the clock for hours as I laid next to Mr. Man in agony. He was clueless to my distress as he laid sound asleep, snoring loudly, probably having a good dream. My pillow often soaked with tears not because my relationship was crumbling before my eyes, but because the joy and peace that I once shared with God had disintegrated at lightning speed. The more I laid in sin, the greater the distance between God and I grew. He never moved away from me. Truth is, I moved away from Him. Here is an excerpt from *Love Was Here All the Time*:

> Romeo and Juliet, Adam and Eve
> Is this love attainable or am I being deceived?
> Throughout this life romantically many have been apart
> But I've never known love ... not real love,
> the kind that emanates from the heart
> What I've known is deceptive, ugly, and cheap.
> The pain, the shame now abiding beneath

Psalm 34:17 (ESV) declares, "When the righteous cry for help, the Lord hears and delivers them out of all their troubles." Not much longer after petitioning God to rescue me from this relationship, God provided the way of escape. Wednesday was my regular off day, the day I usually pampered myself by getting my hair and nails done. This particular Wednesday before leaving for work, Mr. Man asked, as he often did, what plans I had for the day. I told him I would be getting my hair done at ten o'clock, a little grocery shopping, and that I'd probably be out for about four to five hours. My day would later include me performing more of my wifely duties by cooking a nice meal for him as I usually did. (Hmm, now

I'm going to just park that wifey thing right there.) My day was pretty uneventful, and I was on schedule with my plans to serve my king. At least this was what I planned. Dinner would include a big pot of red beans and rice with breaded pork chops. (Remember, I'm a southern girl.) I returned home with grocery bags in hand. I unlocked the door and entered. The heaviness of deception and the smell of betrayal slapped me in the face as I walked in the door. In my soul, I instantly felt something was very wrong. My uneventful day was suddenly about to take a turn. A surprise was waiting for me and not a happy one. What greeted me at the edge of the coffee table was a white piece of notebook paper with my house key lying on top. My eyes immediately welled up as all of my senses began to react. I gazed at my face in the glass top coffee table. Shock and disbelief was all I saw.

As I read the note, my eyes heavy with tears scanning the room, noticing items that belonged to Mr. Man were gone. My stomach began to feel queasy and I felt like I needed to vomit. I walked from room to room, suddenly expecting to no longer see evidence of him living there. The brother was very clear in his note—he was gone. But I guess seeing really is believing. So, I continued to walk from room to room letting my new reality soak in. He even took the cheap bottle of wine given to him by his job for Christmas. I guess he knew me well enough to know that I didn't need it. I wouldn't be drowning my sorrows in a bottle. Instead, I'd be drowning myself in my own tears.

God is the ultimate "super hero." He desires for you to come just as you are, that His transformative power may take root in you, renewing your mind and your spirit.

It did not take long for me to realize that I had been blindsided. I instantly felt like a fool. But I took ownership of this scenario. I allowed Mr. Man to walk into a perfect situation: a fully-furnished home, great conversation, meals every day, his ego stroked, sex and whatever else I thought he needed. Isn't that what we would do for a king? Shouldn't we serve him? I, no one else, made Mr. Man king of my castle. So here I was, devastated. The rug had been yanked from underneath me. What was I to do? After minutes of sobbing, (the real ugly kind of cry) I tried to pull myself together.

I have to admit, I had a real Sybil, psychotic kind of moment (from the movie, *The Exorcist*), and I saw all shades of red. I desperately wanted to react badly. But I was much too broken to do anything but collapse to the floor and sob more. Besides, it became evident to me that this was a well thought-out plan. Reflecting on the previous weeks helped me come to grips with what I knew was true. Mr. Man and I really did not know each other in a way that was genuine and lasting. And although painful, what had occurred was good for both of us. But the question still remains: Why did he have to treat me that way?

That night through my brokenness, I confessed my sin to God. I once again shared everything with Him and asked for forgiveness. Here's where the hard work came in. Life's regimen would now include prayer, fasting, reading the Word, listening to worship music, and watching Christian television. I consumed myself with any and everything that would get me back to God. Over time, I regained my spiritual footing. Together God and I worked through my healing process. God won me back. Here's another nugget for you. God loves you so much; He will always fight for your heart. I had found my best friend again. When I asked, He forgave me instantly. But my brokenness, guilt, and shame would not let me forgive myself. God continued to love me unconditionally through all of it, helping me to discover my vulnerabilities, weaknesses, as well as my strengths. He completely delivered me out of the dark place where I had chosen to reside. This experience and countless others during my life have prompted me to unquestionably trust God as my loving Father. His immeasurable love has paved the way for me to become an authentic woman of God. Here is an excerpt from *Love Immeasurable:*

> Your love is immeasurable
> Your hand of mercy and grace awaits me every morning
> My unworthy heart, my head in hand
> As I struggle on my journey of becoming a Godly woman

Authenticity with God is the building block forming the authentic person that others see in you. With the authority and power God possesses, He can transform you with or without your permission, but He desires your willing and authentic heart. He desires for you to love, seek, worship, and adore Him. He gives us freedom to ask anything of Him from a genuine place. God is the ultimate "super hero." He desires for you to come just as you are, that His transformative power may take root in you, renewing your mind and your spirit. "And do not be conformed to this world, but be ye transformed by the renewing of your mind, that you may prove what is that good and acceptable and perfect will of God" (Romans 12: 2 NKJV). When we willfully come to God unmasked, frail and flawed, He is able to make the vital changes needed for you to have an impact in the earth and bring Him glory. The word vital was intentionally used in the previous sentence. It suggests something that is of the utmost importance, something that is extremely necessary to occur to bring about a desired result. Doesn't it make sense that the giver and Creator of life is the one to draw out and bring forth everything that allows you to be uniquely you? And He is great at doing it. Every experience in life is used by God to grow you and make you better. Here is an excerpt from Love Found Me:

I awaken to love
Good morning, it's a new day
Love embraces me, feeds me and sends me on my way
I look over my shoulder and there you are … love, sweet love
Loving me every step of life's journey

CHAPTER THREE

Becoming Authentic in Love

*A*s I started to write this chapter, my mind started to swirl with the thought of love and the varied ways to describe the word and its French counterpart *amour*. A euphoric feeling instantly took me on a journey of adventure. In the midst of writing, my mind traveled across continents from the hustle and bustle of Atlanta, Georgia to the romantic streets of Paris, France. My final destination would be La Rotonde, a famous French café. I grabbed an outdoor table where I could soak up the sun and observe the culture of this quant city and the diversity of the people passing by. As the waiter approached me, I smiled as if I were the leading lady in the romantic story of the century awaiting my Prince Charming. My request to this gracious lad was simple. "I'd like one cup of amour." Doesn't the sound of that just make your eyes twinkle like stars? What can compare to the undeniable, unquenchable, audacious power of love? When you grasp the magnitude of love, understanding its depth becomes easy. I enjoyed puppy love as a teenager and I believe I have experienced real love at least once in my life. I recall the feeling it gave me, sort of like I was walking on air floating through existence. In some instances, it made me feel strong and larger than life like Wonder Woman or some other kind of super hero bursting out of a phone booth (perhaps I watch too much TV...I chuckle).

The love of God is what real love's about.

All of these feelings are genuine in what they portray. But as you can see from the previous chapter, some forms of love may be met with challenges. Nevertheless, it is what the Bible speaks about love that makes it so beautiful and something most people long to experience. Love unites. It forgives, it hopes, and it gives. It makes you dream, and it sustains you while you pursue your dreams. It upholds you when your heart is overcome with pain and gives you peace when you're feeling distressed. Love reassures you that "no weapon formed against you shall prosper" (Isaiah 54:17 NKJV). You will overcome with love. When love steps in, it allows you to extend yourself beyond your own thoughts and abilities. It fills you with a heart of compassion for others. Love changes people and situations. Oh, the power of love. It can overcome everything that is broken in our world. "Love bears all things, believes all things, and hopes all things. Love never fails" (1 Corinthians 13: 7-8 NKJV).

The miracle of God is love and the essence of love is God. When I think about the essence of something, my mind quickly references "the qualities that make a thing what it is" (Merriam Webster, 2016). It's my belief that God's Spirit dwelling on the inside brings about an outward display of affection visible for all to see and experience. So, what is love? Once again, I must rely on my trusted friend Merriam Webster and its description of the word. Love is "a strong affection for a person." Merriam Webster's description is simple but profound, suggesting a degree of affection that is meaningful and enduring. I guess that explains why love is so magical. It has a power, influence, and supernatural ability to take you to another place by the mere thought of it. My escape to the streets of Paris might also suggest that these feelings and emotions are exclusive to romantic love. But that thought would be inaccurate. God can't be limited to one emotion or mode of thinking. Have you ever purchased something that stated one-size-fits-all? That's God. He and the love that originates in Him fits every person and every scenario. God's love is available any place and any time. Here is another excerpt from *Love Was Here All the Time*:

> The love of God
> is what real love's about.
> It soothes every hurt and erases all doubt
> Always reassuring,
> it was real love that has always carried me.
> Time and time and time again,
> It's real love that bore my sin and hopes for my future
> Real love, wholly and completely in Him.

People love various things. We often use this word to describe our feelings toward things that may not be considered of significant importance to others, but they are very important to us. For instance, I love chocolate, anything chocolate from candy to bacon (yes, bacon). If it's covered in chocolate, I am going to eat it and love every minute of doing it. And let me not forget my enchantment with clothes and shoes. I'm a typical woman when it comes to that. And what about my strong affinity for love songs? Who doesn't reminisce with a good love song? Two of my favorite songs of all time are Roberta Flack's *The First Time Ever I Saw Your Face* and Chaka Khan's rendition of *My Funny Valentine*.

Some of you may have never heard these songs before, but they are classics. If you want to know what amour is and what it is capable of doing, just pull these songs up on Pandora or YouTube. Take a listen. In your mind, you too will find yourself escaping to some faraway place, lost in love just as I was in Paris, France. I embrace the warm, fuzzy thoughts and the cozy feeling of romantic love. But what makes my heart smile the most is the freedom of expressing true love when I choose to share my heart with all those deserving of it.

1 Timothy 1:5 (NKJV) reminds us, "Now the purpose of the commandment is love from a pure heart, from a good conscience, and from sincere faith." The enormity of love grabs the attention of everyone. In speaking about becoming authentic in love, there is only one path that I believe can be pursued. Remember, authenticity is centered in God. This kind of genuine offering of emotion cannot be given or received void of Him, for He is love. Over the years, I've become familiar with varying types of love that one may experience. There is eros, philia, and agape. To fully understand love and its role in genuinely giving and receiving it, we must first look into these three varied types.

Authentic love is founded on truth and must be launched from a place of truth.

According to *The Philosophy of Love* (2016) by A. Moseley, eros is often associated and used within sexual contents driven by intense desire and passion. Philia can be identified through various forms of acknowledgment, gratitude, and devotion. Agape love is a Godly form of love, brotherly love that is extended to all mankind. Many have termed agape love as the highest or greatest form because it is selfless and encompasses all of who God is.

Agape love is pure. A very moving demonstration of agape love was God's sacrificial offering of His beloved son, Jesus Christ for mankind's sin. John 3:16-17 (NIV) beautifully describes God's love for us, "For God so loved the world that he gave His only begotten Son, that whoever believes in Him should not perish but have everlasting life." Here is an excerpt from *Love Immeasurable*:

> Made in your image and likeness too
> At times, difficult to be an example of you
> Your mercy and grace are new every morn
> It's your immeasurable love that my soul depends on

Love can be seen and experienced in every facet of life. As a neonatal nurse, I have had the privilege of witnessing many births. Nothing compares to the instantaneous display of love from a mom or dad to their newly born child. After the birthing process, there is a short period of separation when the new arrival must be examined by the medical staff. From time to time, this period has been met with a small bit of anxiety from the proud new parents. The distress seen is understandable because their wait has been long and the separation, though brief, may feel like an eternity. It then becomes very clear that nothing matches the depth of love that a parent has for their child. But God lovingly allowed His only son to be separated from Him and removed from glory that He (the Son) may redeem us back to the Father (God). Can you imagine what God felt knowing He would be separated from His dearly beloved son? What a display of pure, genuine love!

I've had to grow and mature into living a *Be Authentic Evermore* kind of life. For many years after becoming a mature adult, I battled with body image issues. I struggled with self-love. Somewhere along the line, I bought into the idea that being thin was hot and anything other than being thin was not. I am a curvy girl. Even when I wore a cute size six, I still looked larger than the average size six chick because I have big thighs. Day in and day out, I looked in the mirror and I hated what I saw. I complained constantly. "My thighs are too big and my hips are too wide." Talk about a mess. I was a real complaining Emma. I needed to interject with a bit of humor here as I reflect on the past and who I used to be. This oppressed state of mind was so heavy and burdensome that my displeasure was obvious to friends and loved ones. At times, it became challenging for them to be in my company because of my negative energy. It was difficult for others to fathom where this complaint originated when what they saw was a beautiful and wonderfully made woman of God.

But all I could see was failure in me. Somehow I adopted a mindset that God must have gotten it wrong when He created me. As I sit here now writing what God has placed on my heart, I ask the question: How on earth could I have possibly shared myself with others in an authentic manner when I was so displeased with who I was? When I looked in the mirror, I failed to recognize God's blessing staring back at me. I completely misinterpreted God's concept of beauty allowing an ungrateful heart to have full reign over my thoughts and emotions. A lack of gratitude blocked out all of the wonderful attributes that come together to make me who I am. Years have passed, and God has allowed me to do more hard work in rediscovering my inner beauty. Many days I looked in the mirror empathetically stating, "Hello, beautiful" to the girl that looked back at me, often repeating this statement over and over until my spirit leaped inside of me, and I truly felt and believed what I was saying. Here is an excerpt from *Help Me to See*:

> Help me to see
> The beautiful and wonderfully made me
> The woman you created
> How come when I look in the mirror I see her?
> I see a full butt and big thighs, a wide nose, hair that doesn't know if it wants to be kinky or curly, I see her ...
> You created me in YOUR image and you've given me YOUR heart
> When I look in the mirror she is all I see, I don't see you, I don't see me

Affirming what God says about me was my therapy. It often made me chuckle, but it was a necessary step in my discovery and recovery process. I am reminded by Paul, the writer of Philipians 1:6 (NLT), "And I am certain that God, who began the good work in you, will continue His work until it is finally finished on the day Jesus Christ returns." God is always working on our behalf, working all things together for our good. I look at that girl in the mirror now, and I smile back at her. I love her and she loves me, curves, hips, thighs and all. I still try to maintain a comfortable weight with a pretty decent diet and regular exercise. But I am not the girl I used to be. My oppression with body image issues is finally gone. Every now and then, the enemy tries to creep in, taking me back to that place of discontentment. But I am more aware of his schemes and tricks now. I handle him by going back to the mirror, posing, taking a good look at myself from all angles, saying once again, "Hello, beautiful."

Sharing love with others begins with a true, genuine love of self.

One of my most memorable experiences has to do with my encounter with a homeless man and an unforgettable display of agape love. It was during the winter season, and I was hastily trying to get to work early enough to soothe my chilled body with a warm cup of hot chocolate. Traffic was flowing well on Interstate 85 south in downtown Atlanta. If my estimations were correct, I would arrive at work timely and have ten or fifteen minutes to spare before my shift began. But as I exited the interstate and approached the red light, I saw a homeless man and a dog up ahead. The man began to walk toward my truck, his eyes meeting mine. There was something so drawing about his sky blue eyes, sort of like the magnetic pull when you encounter authenticity. He had captured my attention.

Suddenly, the minutes I would have to spare along with that delicious cup of hot chocolate I eagerly anticipated loss their importance. I pulled to the side of the road and rolled my window down. I was immediately greeted with the frigid temperature of this cold, wintry day and a smile from a man holding a sign with the word "hungry" written on it. His smile seemed so genuine like the sudden smile a baby gives while they sleep. It was pure. Although my obligations would keep me from becoming completely swept away by this stranger, I was instantly engaged with him and for a short time, lost in the moment. I glanced at my watch. As I handed him the few dollars I had in my wallet, I asked him if he knew of a shelter nearby where he could go to get out of the cold temperatures. He smiled at me and said, "I have my best friend with me." As his smile met mine, I remember thinking this was odd (talk about a true display of looking out for man's best friend). Something else that struck me was he smiled a lot. He was a homeless man, hungry with an obvious shortage of clothes to keep him warm during this winter season, and he was smiling. I asked again if he knew of a shelter nearby where he could go to get out of the cold temperatures. He looked at his dog and gazed back at me. He gave me a quirky smile, sort of like when you are up to something, as he in turn answered my question with a question. He asked "What is dog spelled backwards?" Right away, I realized who he was referencing. I responded, "God." He looked confidently at me stating, "We'll be fine" as he turned toward his friend, the dog. I glanced at my watch again and informed him that I needed to leave. As I drove away, I found myself looking back through my rearview mirror attempting to get another glance at him. My soul had been touched. A brief authentic encounter and display of agape love with a homeless man would forever be etched in my heart. You'll hear more about him as you read on.

God desires for all of us to love ourselves and others in a real way. Sharing love with others begins with a true, genuine love of self. The second commandment found in Mark 12:31 (NKJV) reminds us "You shall love your neighbor as yourself." There are countless distractions in the world today and a quiet subtleness that the enemy is using to camouflage his perverted lies and schemes. The truth of God's Word has been distorted and the reality of individual uniqueness in the minds of women and men continues to slip away. You must know who and *whose* you are. See yourself as God's special and unique creation. Dismiss anything contrary to this truth. Many have bought into the enemy's deceptive devices that tell us how we should look, what we should wear, and how we should act. Deception is void of God and His character and so are the enemy's deceptive tactics. As a result, we treat ourselves and others in ways that undermine the love and perfect will of God. Suicide, drug abuse, depression, low self-esteem, and isolation, just to name a few, arise from a deceitful spirit. Here is an excerpt from *I Can't Lose*:

> But just when I thought I had no hope, my Heavenly Father stepped in
> Your life, your existence too important to me
> Before you were born, I mapped out your complete destiny
> And when I couldn't see and thought I had to choose
> My Heavenly Father said, "Rest my child, I love you, I'll walk in those shoes."

Authenticity and love appear to have taken a backseat within our society. But do not be dismayed by what you see. Deuteronomy 3:24 (NKJV) speaks to God's sovereignty (supreme power and authority). "O Lord God, You have begun to show Your servant Your greatness and Your mighty hand, for what god is there in heaven or on earth who can do anything like Your works and Your mighty deeds." Life throws us curve balls from time to time, but the sovereignty of God should never be questioned. He allows things to happen with a divine purpose and plan in mind. His thoughts are far greater than ours, so His methodology may not always be understood. But success in life requires ARMing yourself, to **Align** with God, allowing Him to bring forth your authenticity. You must simply trust Him. As God reigns in you, so shall authenticity and love reign in you. **Relinquish** your will. Allow Him to lead your life. Sit back and enjoy the ride. Seek clarity, direction and **Move** in your purpose. Watch God show out.

CHAPTER FOUR

Becoming Authentic in Relationships

In writing this book, it seemed fitting to address becoming authentic in relationships after laying the groundwork with becoming authentic with God and becoming authentic in love. Everything good that pertains to your very existence is birthed and evolves out of Godly love. This includes relationships. Personal and professional relationships help shape who we become during our lifetime. Those individuals whom we deem special or have had positive interactions with bring out wonderful character traits in us. Contrary to popular belief, the not so positive exchanges bring out hidden treasures in us as well.

You don't know you need to be washed, purified, and cleaned up unless you realize you are dirty.

God is the master strategist. His sovereignty is proof that He uses every person and circumstance to bring about a desired end. Our best and worse relationships give us a snapshot of who we are and who we will become. The picture may not always be pretty. But it often takes revealing the good, bad, and ugly junk that has taken root within our hearts to bring about meaningful change. I smile at God's presence in my life. I thank Him for moments of reflection and the evidence of His marvelous work in me. These beautiful moments make my heart leap with joy because I am His. But every moment of my life has not been good and every reflective thought has not made my heart dance.

I have had selfish and unkind moments, more than I care to recall. What do you do when God's DNA has not been very apparent in your behavior? Not a pretty thought, but there is hope in Him. Here's where you have to put your big girl panties on. When these moments of reflection rear their ugly head, I own my foolishness and wayward acts. I talk to God openly and honestly. I repent with a sincere heart. I listen to Him, take note, and gain from the experience. I then move from that place realizing God wastes nothing. He'll take your mishap and allow you to bless someone else with your experience at the right time, if you are willing. Over time, I've learned to thank God for those deeply penetrating moments of thought. This may be a hard statement to digest, but hear me in the spirit. You don't know you need to be washed, purified, and cleaned up unless you realize you are dirty. You aren't aware of your need for repair until you get a bird's eye view of your brokenness. When your soul is not full of God and other things have rule over you, sharing yourself from a real place becomes questionable. King David, a true renaissance man and one to be admired, accurately sang my sentiments in Psalm 51:10-13 (NKJV), "Create in me a clean heart, O God, and renew a steadfast spirit within me. Do not cast me away from Your presence, and do not take Your Holy Spirit from me. Restore to me the joy of Your salvation, and uphold me by Your generous Spirit. I will teach transgressors Your ways, and sinners shall be converted to You." Here is an excerpt from *More of You*:

More of you with a repentant heart
Envelope me in your love, Lord fill each part
More of Your Word, Your Spirit, and Your Presence too
Rescue me, save me, Lord I need more of you

Relationships are formed. The authenticity shared in them involves an exchange or transfer much like the stuff we remember from chemistry class. If you are like me, you want to forget chemistry. But who can forget that unique science that involves formulas and the sharing or transfer of chemicals, electrons, or molecules to produce something new and different. I remember chemistry well and all of the growing pains associated with it. How I loved to hate, and hated to love the concept of this complex science. But for the sake of all of us becoming authentic in relationships, I will take a trip down memory lane. Let's think about the forming of a relationship like we would think about the formulated chemical exchange involved in baking a cake. My love for anything chocolate might make it fair for you to assume that I could have an affinity for chocolate cake. Assumption correct. I love chocolate cake!

Now, there are several ingredients needed to make the rich, delectable kind of chocolate cake that I love to eat. You need flour, cocoa powder, milk (I use heavy cream—the good stuff), salt, eggs, shortening, baking soda, baking powder, vanilla, sugar, and butter. Blending these various ingredients is essential to the mixing process when attempting to bake a cake that will satisfy. For instance, flour needs to be sifted and milk slowly added in parts. Some ingredients need to be added at the start, while others are added in the middle and others at the end. What is clear is that a systematic approach to blending these ingredients along with other necessary steps must be followed. The end result is something enticing to your palette. Have you ever tried to bake a cake without the required ingredients listed, such as no eggs, water, or milk? I hope not. Without an agent to bind all of the dry ingredients together, you are just left with a dry, floury mess.

Relationships are formed in a very similar way. Indulge me for a bit longer as I make an interesting comparison between relationships and the baking of a cake. Becoming authentic in relationships involves God. He is much like the flour in a cake, a fundamental component for your relationship success. Shortening creates moisture, much like love does when it saturates your motives and intentions. Wholeness of self provides a structure for nourishing relationships sort of like eggs do. Cocoa powder gives flavor and color, similar in the way that opening ones heart to possibilities in relationships can. Baking soda and baking powder share a sisterhood as respect and trust do. The two together bring forth the depth that is necessary to build something lasting and memorable. Time can be compared to salt, providing that additional welcomed kick needed for longevity. If you want to enhance your relationship, as vanilla enhances chocolate cake, just step up the communication. That includes listening more. For a bit of sweetener, go on, pucker up. Sprinkle your sugar with a healthy dose of passion. To keep things smooth like butter and on an even keel, laugh a little. Scratch that! Laugh a lot! And last but surely not least, for that crispy, solid edge that all relationships need, always be kind.

*Feelings of loneliness bring such
sadness and heaviness of heart.*

This journey of self-discovery and healing has been amazing and my growth and development to living authentically has been so rewarding. But as I mentioned earlier, I have had selfish moments and have been unfair and unkind at times. I have been guilty of dibbling and dabbling with those that were not in a position to be in a relationship with me. What does that mean, Bre? It means that I have played the role of the mistress or what is otherwise known as the other woman. This next statement does not excuse or justify this intolerable behavior, but it needs to be stated. Loneliness, brokenness, and emptiness can make you selfish, desperate, and unkind. Sad, but true. The precious time spent involved in meaningless relationships cannot be regained. The jagged edge wounds that develop from such behavior takes time for all parties to heal. The deception that gives rise to such injury and heartache toward those who are completely innocent and undeserving is unacceptable. For this, I am truly sorry.

Admission can be difficult. As I began to write this book, I realized *Be Authentic Evermore* is not just about me becoming a better version of myself. It is about God's purpose and plan for me, you, you, and you. It's all about what He has destined for us, including the manifestation of all of our hopes and dreams. Here's good news: "If we confess our sins, He is faithful and just to forgive us our sins and to cleanse us from all unrighteousness" (1 John 1:9 KJV). God's Word is true. He has used every misstep I've ever made for my good. It is my prayer that He gets the glory from it all.

Do you remember the homeless man I so passionately spoke of in the previous chapter? I had no idea what was in store for me after my chance encounter with him. You'll hear me refer to him as "my angel" from this point on. Visions of him and his dog were implanted in my mind. All I could do was hope for a second encounter that would be as magical as the first. During this time, I worked the weekend night shift at South Fulton Medical Center located in East Point, Georgia. Saturdays and Sundays were routine for me. I slept most of each day and I wore the same attire to work: white scrubs. I usually picked up take out from the same place and my route to work remained unchanged as well. The big difference in my weekend routine now was the presence of an angel.

My eyes lit up as I exited Interstate 85 toward Cleveland Avenue, the street where I initially met him. I could see the dog walking in the distance as I approached the end of the exit ramp. I pulled to the side of the road and watched as my angel appeared from underneath bent up boxes and a torn tent. Our smiles met as he walked toward my truck. He recognized me, and it appeared he was pleased to see me. I rolled the window down and with the excitement of a kid at Christmas I stated, "I brought you something." I had picked up a winter hat and a pair of gloves for him from the store a few days earlier. This particular day, on my drive into work, I grabbed a quick bite for him and me to eat. His hand lightly touched mine as he reached for the things I had for him. His eagerness to chat was evident as he hurriedly placed the items down on a pile of dirty clothes laying in the grass. There was ease and comfort in our dialogue, so I felt relaxed asking him questions about his life. He didn't seem to mind. I was curious to know if he had family in the city. Was there someone I could call or reach out to on his behalf? Maybe there was some chance his family was unaware of his plight. So many thoughts were running through my mind. In this limited amount of time, I wanted to gather as much information as I could about him. He shared that he had a wife and a daughter but that was all he said about them. Curiosity was killing me. I wanted to know more. I wanted to help him. But I didn't push. I figured in time I would get more answers.

Feelings of loneliness bring such sadness and heaviness of heart. It's difficult to find a smile when you feel alone. But somehow in this unfathomable state, my angel appeared at peace with his friend, God and his friend, dog. Throughout our interaction, just like the infamous dancer Ginger Rogers did with her partner Fred Astaire in the 1930s, I followed his lead. Allowing him to be my leading man gave him freedom to ask me questions about myself. He wanted to know pretty generic stuff like did I like my job and did I like dogs. I told him I grew up with dogs and liked them somewhat. I added, "but I love God" as I allowed my mind to take me back to the first question he ever asked me. He looked up with his sky blue eyes meeting the clouds as if He knew God was somewhere up there sitting on the throne watching over him. It seemed safe for us to talk about God and faith. Our worlds so different, but it was common ground for him and me. Honestly, we appeared to be quite enchanted with each other. After ten minutes, I told him I would have to leave for work. As I started my truck, I'll never forget the warm and fuzzy way I felt when he said,

"Goodbye, my friend. Have a good night." I waved and replied, "Goodbye, my friend."

On my off days, my mind often wondered if he and his dog had anything to eat, or if they had found a better place to lay their heads. Had my angel touched other lives like he had touched mine? Would I continue to be impacted by him and where would this all lead? I found myself looking forward to Saturday and Sunday evenings because I knew he would be in the same spot, hopefully waiting for me. The Bible urges us, "Do not forget to show hospitality to strangers, for by doing so some people have shown hospitality to angels without knowing it" (Hebrews 13:2 NIV). In anticipation of having more memorable encounters with my angel, I began to gather more things for him. I bought socks, mittens, a wool lumberjack shirt, and a fleece blanket. I would no longer wonder if he and his dog were warm. I was doing my small part to ensure they were going to be.

Working the night shift will cause you to eat more than normal. At least I did to keep myself from walking into walls during the night. There is something so unnatural about working throughout the night. I never got used to it. Staying on schedule and following my regimen hinged on how much sleep I had gotten prior to getting ready for the night's work. If I maintained the schedule as planned, my normal routine included stopping by the nearby Piccadilly, a cafeteria-type buffet, to pick up dinner for Saturday and Sunday. My choices always included a salad, meat, starch, two vegetables, and a dinner roll. I needed every bit of nourishment to keep me alert and moving through two o'clock to five o'clock a.m. hours. But things were a little different now. Instead of picking up two dinner plates for takeout, I began to pick up three. Images of the sign that read "hungry" were vividly etched in my mind. I was limited in what I could do for this man, but his well-being had become important to me. Pretty soon I began to alter my weekend regimen. I needed to allow myself more time to spend with him. It became clear to me that a very unique but real relationship was taking shape. Here is an excerpt from *Lord Send A Revival*:

> Lord send a revival, this world needs it I pray
> So loss and caught up in our own selfish way
> The widow, the orphan, the homeless man on the street
> The insanity of children not having anything to eat

These encounters went on for a little over a month. But as quickly as this homeless man came into my life, my angel disappeared. Sadly, one Saturday evening as I pulled up to our special meeting place, my friend and his dog were no longer there. The boxes and the raggedy tent that once covered him, keeping him out of the cold were gone. There was no evidence of him having ever been there. All that remained was dead grass. Suddenly that corner looked dry and desolate like all the others in the dead of winter. For a brief moment, I thought perhaps he had moved to the opposite side of the interstate. I immediately circled around, looking anxiously for him, wanting desperately to see him or the dog. But they never appeared again. All that was left was the memory of him, his smile, and his faith. Now I am reminded of the special man with the sky blue eyes every time I pass that exit on Interstate 85. Despite fear of the unknown and disappointments in past relationships, God and love allowed me to establish an amazingly authentic relationship with an angel, a homeless man.

What allows the good seeds to grow and bad seeds to dry up are the presence of God and His Word in your life.

Over the years, I have been blessed to establish many lasting relationships. As I think about these connections, one common denominator rests at the center of them all. This commonality is authenticity. I, like many of you, gravitate to people whose genuineness radiates from the things they say and do. When I have the pleasure of experiencing a mental and spiritual attraction between myself and others, I embrace the opportunity. I seize the moment knowing that the soil is rich for growth and the potential to develop a lasting, quality relationship is great. But as I speak on this subject, I'd like to give you a little food for thought. This next bit of information may not be for everyone, but I would be remiss in not touching upon it since we are all on a journey in becoming the best we can be. Our journeys are different, and how we unmask our truth is likely different as well.

I believe the statements I am about to make are important and need to be identified as we delve more into relating to each other in a genuine manner. I pray that you hear my heart as I speak to the interactions we have with other women. Allow yourself to be honest about what your heart speaks as it relates to your female counterparts. God skillfully designed women to embody like characteristics, yet we are so uniquely different. There is priceless information within our likeness and differences. We all have something valuable to offer each other. It's your beauty. It's not outward beauty that attracts, as the world would attempt to make us believe. Instead, it is an inward beauty that you and only you have the exclusive rights to. The exclusivity of your beauty gives you the power to control how, when, and with whom it is shared. Within the pages of this book, I offer my beauty to you in hopes that you are blessed by it. Here is an excerpt from *Sister Friend*:

> My symbol of beauty is my sister-friend
> Not outward beauty as one might quickly assume
> But the inner beauty that a woman of God, covenant sister,
> and true friend might exude
> You know the one that hears pain in your voice
> Even when you're sounding bubbly and upbeat
> Or so you thought
> Our spirits connected

She knows me, she feels me, she loves me

There has been a shift in the atmosphere over the last few decades. Much of what we see, hear, and read from society sets us up for relational failure. I encourage everyone to do your homework and research things that are of importance to you. When we don't take the needed time to gain as much knowledge as we can about things of significance, we do ourselves and others a great disservice. I've learned that I cannot buy into everything I see, hear, and read. With this same mode of thinking, I'd like to touch a little more on things that may become pitfalls to us developing genuine relationships with other women.

I've found this next statement to be a biggie. Simply put, insecurity, jealously, and competition will keep you from being real with others. These distasteful emotions will also hinder your growth and block hidden blessings. Over the years I've had to recognize instances when I was harboring this kind of ugliness. I purposely called it ugliness because it distorts the beauty of who you are in such a way that it is displeasing to the eye.

I not only had to come face to face with it, but I needed to discover the root cause of it. So many experiences in life have lasting effects on us. For me, it's been the disappointments and deception of past relationships that opened the door to insecurity and mistrust. When that door is opened, bad seeds may be planted if we are not careful. Every day, seeds are deposited in our minds from various sources. What allows the good seeds to grow and bad seeds to dry up are the presence of God and His Word in your life. Intimacy with Him keeps you steady when life throws you a blow. He must fill every space, void, and need. The enemy likes to take advantage of any vacancies in your mind and heart, distorting the truth of God's Word. But God wants to safeguard you. God wants you to ARM yourself. Stay close to Him.

When bad seeds happen upon just a smidgen of soil that will allow for growth, it can be unattractive and destructive. Here's a question I've wondered about and have even asked myself at times. What happens when we see an attractive female, have an admiring thought about her and even acknowledge it by saying, "She's pretty." Oddly we end that affirming statement with something negative like, "but her weave is messed up" or "she's too thick!" I understand we may have opinions and thoughts about people and various things, but not every thought needs to be shared. Some fleeting thoughts are meant to do just that, simply pass through the moment. But our thoughts may give us a clue that we are harboring bad seeds.

So, it's important to be honest with yourself. Here's another scenario. What hinders us from celebrating another female's advancement or accomplishments? We are often cool when we are kicking it on the same level, when in our eyes we are equal. But when God steps in, brings increase and opens a door for someone else, we sometimes are left feeling sort of left behind. We must kill these self-defeating thoughts. This behavior is dangerous and counterproductive. It leaves you stagnant and vulnerable to more negativity that may be lurking.

Over the years I have learned not to covet another's blessings, gifts, or talents and to freely celebrate another's accomplishments. What God has done for one, He surely can do for another. He desires to shower us with good gifts, but it's about His timing and His will. Grab hold to the "R" in ARMing yourself. Relinquish your will and trust God for your increase. Here's an excerpt from *Girlfriends*:

> You share your soul, your very heart
> Because girlfriend has your back, every single part
> Or so you thought
> What is that thing that sometimes creeps into the mind of girlfriend?
> Bound by my own issues,
> it keeps me from being genuine

As I mentioned earlier, we can't buy into everything that society says looks, sounds and feels good. We just can't. Learn as much as you can about everything you desire to. You can never have too much knowledge. Knowledge equips you and gives you eagle soaring strength and power. Knowledge also allows you to determine what is good or bad for you. If it cannot benefit you and keep you ARMed, get rid of it. I hope the process of ARMing yourself on your path to greatness has been clear throughout the experiences and stories shared. Here are a few simple tips on how to succeed on your journey. Cultivate your relationship with God, learn from Him and His Word, and bask in His presence. It's in this place where you learn to align, relinquish, and move in Him. The Prophet Jeremiah describes God as a fountain of living waters (Jeremiah 2:13 ESV). The days are moving fast and time is quickly passing. But when you stop and sit with God awhile, authenticity begins to overflow naturally out of you. It creates an aroma that is refreshing and drawing to others.

Since we are growing together, I'd like to touch on male-female relationships as well. I have managed to develop a few lasting friendships with men over the years (when I have had my head on straight). That may sound pretty humorous, but it is true. There have been instances when I've lost my head and attempted to take my interactions with men or my relationship with them into my own hands. At times, I've felt very needy and desperate for someone to love me. If I happened to find myself in the driver's seat on the road to relationship heaven, my foot often took to the gas pedal and vroom, I was off. I could go from zero to one hundred after one date, ready to plan the wedding. Did I consult God about the fella? No. Did I listen for why our paths crossed? No. I just moved in desperation, in my own way and in my own time. I had to get this next statement in my spirit to keep from bumping my head over and over again.

Every man that you encounter is not meant to be your knight in shining armor, your prince, or your Mr. Right. I recall on numerous occasions meeting a guy, engaging in conversation, and maybe even exchanging phone numbers. If I was attracted to him and liked what he had to say, it became very normal, at least to me, to wonder if he was the one. Seriously, Bre? (I chuckle).

In time, I've learned that most of the men in my life were not there for romance at all, but for other reasons that could have been more satisfying and valuable. Time will always reveal what is true. Time helps you see clearly, giving you 20/20 vision. Give time its place in your relationships with men. God is your drum major for life. Stay in step with Him and allow Him to determine the next move and the timing of it. God has given men the power to lead us. Let the fella hear from God and make the move toward something greater if it is part of God's plan. Remember Ginger Rogers from chapter four? She never went wrong with Fred Astaire as her leading man. Here is an excerpt from *The Stranger, My Friend*:

> You came to me a complete stranger.
> God's part of the plan
> My heart joyous and thankful
> Because God had sent me my man
> The one who would love me,
> take care and grow old with me too
> The assumption I made could make a fool out of me and you
> God connects paths and He joins hearts
> But we often miss God's purpose and plan because
> well, we think He's finally sent us our man

There are no words to describe the value and the beauty resulting from honest, genuine relationships. Our lives are distinctively different but parallel in extraordinary ways. Your experience, testimony, and story are not just for you to reflect on or reminisce about. Instead, they should be used to appropriately share as you build relationships with others. It's sort of like building a jigsaw puzzle. When all of the mismatched pieces are connected, what's built is beautiful and complete. But what happens to this array of beauty when pieces are missing and connections can't be made? All you are left with are pieces of a person and not the real essence of who they are.

    It's impossible to build relationships if you won't allow others to see you from a genuine standpoint. I recognize that this can be risky business. Here's a workable solution. Entrust your relationships unto God. Ask Him to reveal all that you need to know as it pertains to others and their place in your life. Petition Him to safeguard your heart. Trust Him to be your Father and friend. Sit back. Work on yourself. Enjoy your progress and embrace change as authenticity takes place in you.

CHAPTER FIVE

Becoming Authentic with Self

Self-awareness and the ability to clearly and honestly evaluate self are essential if one is to live authentically. In the play Hamlet, the character Polonius quoted Shakespeare stating, "This above all, to thine own self be true." One can possibly hide things from family, friends, and those closest to you. But in my experience, when you allow yourself to escape into a real quiet mental and spiritual space, the ability to accurately look at who you are becomes quite easy. "Every way of a man is right in his own eyes, but the Lord weighs the heart" (Proverbs 21:2 ESV). What lies beneath the surface—positive or negative—can never be hidden from God, and it will eventually be brought to light for you and others to see.

I enlisted a book coach in writing this book. I call her Madame Coach. I remember our first session as if it were yesterday. After giving Madame Coach the title of this book and

Be Authentic Evermore

a brief synopsis of what I envisioned for it, she asked me why I thought I could write on this subject. She later followed that question with how do you maintain an authentic evermore life? My answer was short, sweet, and to the point. I stated, "I have always been able to look at myself and be honest about what I see. When I've been happy about what I see, I may give God two thumbs up for giving me pretty nice character traits such as compassion, strength, and thoughtfulness. But when I've been disappointed with what I have chosen to become, there's no need to give God two thumbs up. It's not His fault. Instead, I just give it to Him, whatever it is—flaws, issues, cares and concerns—all of it. I am comfortable going to Him in confidence confessing my shortcomings. For I am sure He is the only One that can make my crooked paths straight.

It's easy to recognize those admirable attributes that make us who we are. But we may find great difficulty in coming to terms with the imperfect areas that also play an important role in how we progress and evolve in life. When you are in tune with self and even more in tune with God, He gives you the capacity to identify those things that the enemy uses to trap you, keep you bound, and sabotage His purpose and plans for you.

God has done some of His best work in the imperfect lives of many.

I believe getting to know self is a normal, continuous process that begins when we are young and continues throughout life. In my years as a neonatal ICU nurse, I've cared for more babies than I can count. It's interesting watching their little personalities evolve from day to day. Who could ever forget Ms. Thang from my early days in nursing? She was a premature baby girl, born at twenty-six weeks gestation. For those of you who may not be familiar with this terminology, it means she was born fourteen weeks too early. She weighed a little over two pounds at birth, but her personality was larger than life. She was known as the feisty baby of the nursery owning up to her name, Ms. Thang.

She commanded your attention with her spunky attitude. She knew what she liked and didn't like. She preferred to sleep on her side and was most comfortable when her area was dimly lit. She wasn't crazy about getting a bath, although she appeared to be soothed by the feel of warm water on her body. She loved attention and seemed to be captivated when I sang songs to her. This was our special moment together. It allowed us to communicate in an unexplainable sort of way. Her eyes would become big and bright as I sang songs like "Jesus Loves the Little Children" and "Twinkle Twinkle Little Star." Her tiny lips puckering intermittently as if she wanted to say something back to me. But when Ms. Thang didn't have her way, she pouted and stared at you like you were an alien. Tears often accompanied those stares. It was the combination of her tears and her stares that would make your heart melt. And after you picked your heart up off the floor, this little angel girl usually got her way. Even at this very early age, she knew what brought her pleasure and what did not.

In becoming authentic with self, it is important to align with God's standards for authentic living. The Bible is our behavioral manual and God is our standard of excellence. On a daily basis, you make the choice to be God's ambassador and live in the manner that He has outlined. As you mature and walk with Him, His standard becomes your standard. As I mentioned earlier, our imperfections play a role in how we grow and how our lives take shape, both physically and spiritually. God has done some of His best work in the imperfect lives of many. Here are a few examples to validate this statement. Did you know King David was an adulterer and murderer, Jacob was a liar and stole from his brother, Rahab was a prostitute, and Samson had a tremendous weakness for women? But all of these biblical characters flawed and sketchy in their own way were used by God. In time, each of them had to not only recognize their weaknesses but acknowledge them and the sovereignty of the Almighty. You and I must walk this same path if God is to get the glory out of our lives. When you are real with God, He showers you with grace and prepares you for your next level.

But we must be ready to ARM ourselves for change.

Do you remember my struggle with body image issues from chapter three? Believe it or not, when I was in my twenties, I was extremely confident in who I was. My cute, curvy body could stop traffic and I knew it. But failed relationships eventually chipped away at my confidence. I battled with the thoughts of not being pretty, fit and fine, or sexy enough. I began to own all of the relational failures that had occurred in my life. My mind believed I had done something horribly wrong in all of them. I thought maintaining my figure, wearing sexy revealing clothes, cooking lovely meals straight out of *Bon Appetit* magazine, giving gifts (nice gifts), and sharing the most intimate part of me (my body) was a workable formula for success. But in doing all of that, I still failed to sustain a lasting relationship. With each disappointment, I felt more and more incomplete and disliked myself more and more. Why did I always take ownership of these failed relationships despite the deception that was common in all of them? Over time, the thoughts I had would not only become self-destructive for me but exhausting as well. Here is an excerpt from *Help Me to See*:

> What happened when he chose her over me?
> What has society done, screaming thin is in?
> And their hair down my back makes me pret-tee
> What did Daddy do when he never said,
> "You are so beautiful?"
> And Mama was too busy being mom and dad that she never shared
> Your Word that says

Be Authentic Evermore

> I am fearfully and wonderfully made
> The apple of Your eye, beautiful in Your sight

In those earlier days, I was not mature enough spiritually to fully grasp the magnitude of my inner beauty. So, I struggled for years studying women and not trusting men, trying to figure out this dysfunction. I worked out faithfully, not necessarily for health reasons, but because I needed to regain my curvy body. This was the body and size I was so confident would grab the attention of male onlookers. This very unbalanced way of thinking continued despite the years. Maturity in life happens, but it is not time sensitive. The level in which maturity develops is a response to multiple factors. The maturation process does not always match up chronologically or simply put with age. Here I was an older woman, immature in my thoughts about some aspects of my life and God's truth about me. I was disillusioned within myself and the root cause was deeply embedded. A breakthrough was desperately needed. I was going crazy like a dog chasing its tail. I still needed to recognize my greatest asset was my inner beauty.

Little did I know, my breakthrough was on the horizon. God is loving and gracious, always giving us what we need. He provides so much time for reflection, giving you time to figure things out. As we pull ourselves together through life's challenges, He makes the necessary changes to get us where we need to be. But we must be ready to ARM ourselves for change. We must be ready for a better way of living. One unforgettable night, in my desperation to be free, God heard my plea. I remember thinking back on the romantic relationships of my past. I also remember shedding tears over the disappointment in them. I couldn't believe with all of my best efforts (you remember those listed a few paragraphs up), that I had failed again, again, and again. How could love escape me time after time? I was baffled by the thought that not one of the men in my past saw my real beauty. Here's another moment of clarity, another 20/20 vision moment for you. In all of my past relationships, I got what I presented. Please enjoy the inspirational clip *What I Present*:

> My baby doll skirt, high-heel shoes,
> and everything else that's revealed
> I'm dressed to impress. Who? I ask myself.
> I stride past you slowly, so you may get a glimpse
> Your attention is what I'm after, so with every attempt
> I draw you in
> This ain't a dress rehearsal, I only have one chance
> First impressions are lasting and happen in one glance
> I draw you in
> Your respect I want, but I'm going about it in the wrong way
> A set up for you to play with my mind and my heart
> The physical you see, your lust driving you to me
> I let you see more than you should
> I've let you in
> Now each day thereafter, I battle trying to escape your
> lust and this reoccurring sin
> I try to rewind, come get to know me

> But you can't, still caught up in the physical you see
> I let you in, but you missed my real beauty

That night I cried a lot. I prayed and I cried, I cried and I prayed. Feeling so weary and worn, without hesitation I looked to God as my source of strength. There's nothing strange about looking to Him for comfort when you are at a low point. In Psalm 121:1 (KJV), King David directs our thoughts when he writes, "I will lift up mine eyes unto the hills, from whence cometh my help." In my despair, God held me close and I eventually cried myself to sleep. Throughout the night, He comforted me and ministered to my broken heart. The next morning, I awakened to the sound of a beautiful melody in my ear. I was not fully awake. I was in a semi-sleep state. But in this state I could hear the sound of beautiful music in my car. And as I was lying in bed, this melodic sound would begin to penetrate my soul. It was a familiar song that expresses the undeniable love of the Father God to His child. What God was relaying to me was clear. It was a remarkable expression of His unconditional, undying love for me. At a time when I needed to feel loved more than ever, God reassured me as He has done many times before, that I am forever loved by Him.

"So if the Son sets you free, you will be free indeed"
(John 8:36 NIV)

I have heard God's love preached countless times. I have felt His love and even spoken of it. But for whatever reason, His love had not become fully alive to me. The years of despair over the men I was involved with would make this statement true. But on this night, my true Prince Charming would not only rescue me, but awaken me to this indisputable fact. My hands were wide open as I grabbed hold of this truth and clung to it for dear life. On this most crucial night, God changed things for me. He transformed my thinking and renewed my mind after a very authentic moment with Him. Always remember, "So if the Son sets you free, you will be free indeed" (John 8:36 NIV). Here is an excerpt from *Joy*:

> Your peace, Your love You give to me
> Calmness, void of strife,
> Everyday I am free
> At day's end I follow You as You lead me
> Beside still waters, my soul You restore

When I embarked on this journey of writing *Be Authentic Evermore*, I have to admit I was terrified. Throughout my school days I believed I had enough skills to compose a pretty good paper, but I never considered myself a writer. And the thought of becoming an author never ever entered my mind. I had previously written *Melodeez of the Heart (MOTH)*, a collection of poetry and I feel really good about what I produced. But compiling MOTH did not require as much attention to detail that composing *Be Authentic Evermore* has. However,

I am aligned with God. I have relinquished my will and I am moving in purpose. I am ARMed and I have given God a resounding yes. So, I sat every day attentive to Him, writing every word He spoke, and sharing the most sacred parts of myself with you. When I think about the journey I am on, I often laugh. In my amazement, I find myself asking God the same silly question. "Seriously, God?" When my mind allows me to grasp what He has given me, a feeling of exhilaration floods my soul. I pinch myself because it just doesn't seem real. I am an author and you are reading my story. Who would have thought? (I chuckle)

Fear has risen from time to time challenging me in my quest to remain transparent and authentic in my sharing. But my determination to please God, live purposefully, and provide you with a life-changing story is the fuel for me to continue without hesitation. As I read over previous chapters, I smile at the woman I have become and the courage I have to live each day from a genuine place. I now embrace my curvy, grown woman body. I might even still be able to stop a car or two, although I'm not interested in trying. I am more concerned about being a worthy example of God. My season of change has come and every day I praise Him for it. "To all who mourn in Israel, he will give a crown of beauty for ashes, a joyous blessing instead of mourning, festive praise instead of despair. In their righteousness, they will be like great oaks that the LORD has planted for his own glory" (Isaiah 61:3 NLT).

CHAPTER SIX

Becoming Authentic in Happiness

Fleeting moments of happiness have come and gone, but I've never known what real happiness felt like until now. If you asked anyone (who knows me well) the question, "What would make Bre most happy?" many of them, if not all, would have the same response. I've never kept my desire to be a wife and mother a secret. As a young girl growing up, I, like many of you, fantasized about Prince Charming one day sweeping me off of my feet. And after my fairy tale rescue, I would fall madly in love and live happily ever after with the Prince, two kids, and maybe a dog. It's funny how we hold on to those girlish fantasies even as we mature.

If I somehow finally managed to kiss a prince instead of a frog, I would indeed be overjoyed. But being a mother would just send my heart to the moon. Perhaps, it's the fresh smell that only a baby has that I love. Or maybe it's the twinkle in their eyes that has captivated me for years. In a world full of discontentment and chaos, it's the innocence that only a baby can possess that sometimes makes me feel safe. I could probably create a laundry list of reasons why I have such an incredible affinity for these amazing little creatures. No one reason stands out more than any other. My thought has always been that motherhood is an extraordinary gift from God. It's a gift that I desperately craved for years. My first glimpse at motherhood came when I was seventeen. Here is an excerpt from *Encounters That Cost*:

> Caught up, a first encounter leaves me with a life within
> Ten fingers, ten toes, on me that life would depend
> A myriad of emotions—love, fear, excitement, and joy
> The nurturer in me awakened, present, and well accounted for
> But I was a child, how on earth would I begin to address this first encounter turned calamity?
> And how would I break this shocking news to my very proud family?

I come from a long line of proud individuals. My great-grandmother was a pillar of strength, successfully raising eight children. All eight of them were hard-working, ambitious, and oh so proud. Mama, my grandmother, was the oldest of eight. She was the epitome of a woman. She always could provide whatever was needed and everything she put her hands to was done in excellence. Adoration is all that was seen when Mama looked at or talked about her grandchildren. We never did any wrong in her eyes. My mother, Mommie as she is called, was the spitting image of Mama in character. Mommie's actions throughout my life have made it crystal clear that she wanted nothing but the best for my siblings and I. She has sacrificed so much for us over the years and she still does. Her love is unquestionable to this very day. Her proud persona is still a mark of the long line of strong, classy women and men who have helped to shape my family's existence. This generational display of pride would be my solid rock growing up, and the stumbling block that would change my life forever. Here is another excerpt from *Encounters That Cost*:

> Six, eight, twelve weeks, not much longer to hide
> Be careful with your secrets when you begin to confide
> in those that can't relate to the love you feel for the life growing on
> the inside
> Before it's too late my secret was known,
> and everything instantly erased for the life and the love I had known
> Mama's love for me said, "You must finish school."
> I wonder, would her response have been different if she only knew
> the years of depression and pain I'd have to suffer through?
> A trip to the clinic and like smoke that life was gone
> But at seventeen years old,
> it was Mama to care for me and her I had to depend on

After that unforgettable day, a conversation regarding this ordeal never came up in my house. My immaturity during this time did not allow me to fully understand the magnitude of what had occurred. But my heart and my body knew I had loss something. My mind and emotions began sweeping everything under the rug as if those ten tiny fingers and ten tiny toes never existed. But they did.

After a few weeks, I became a regular teen again looking forward to the arrival of fall and my entry into college. The lack of conversation and information about my untimely pregnancy and the consequences resulting from it would later prove to be a missed step. Three years later, I found myself back in the same predicament. A missed menstrual cycle and a few mornings of nausea and vomiting would confirm in my mind what my body already knew. I had become pregnant again. Here's another excerpt from *Encounters That Cost*:

> Years passed, another encounter, another life within
> My soul tormented and full of shame at my reoccurring sin
> Without much thought, the decision I'd make
> Succumbing to fear, brokenness, and unresolved pain
> My eyes full of tears as I showed up at the clinic once again

Needless to say, years of unresolved pain and brokenness led to extreme sadness, although this sadness was something I hid very well. I continued to live a normal life and experience fleeting moments of happiness. But the thought of my unborn babies remained and the mother's love that I instantly felt during my short encounter with them was unescapable. More years would pass and the sadness just increased. After becoming a career woman and finding my niche in the neonatal intensive care unit (NICU), I often made comparisons with my insatiable desire to be a mother and my duty to care for babies in the ICU. What irony? Was this some sort of joke God was playing on me? Some of my most intense conversations with Him have been about this painful part of my life. I am sure He has heard my cry and plea for answers. Knowing God as I have come to know Him, I believe He has made attempts to provide comfort and the much needed answers. But more often than not, my unquenchable thirst for happiness as a mother did not allow me to feel or hear God as it related to this heartfelt matter.

Is anything too hard for the Lord?"
(Genesis 18:12-14 NIV)

Since I was in my early twenties, I battled with fibroids and endometriosis. Over the course of years, the incapacitating pain and heavy menstrual cycles every month would be almost too much to bear. I had no idea what the presence of these foreign bodies were doing to my female organs. My treatment regimen over the years would include hormone injections, birth control pills, pain medication, and when all else failed, surgery. As a nurse, I was well aware of the possible complications associated with surgical procedures, but the risk of surgery could never compare with the risk of never being called mommy. So, I endured not one or two, not three but four surgeries always hoping that time would be the last time. At this point, you may be wondering what all of this has to do with becoming authentic in happiness. It seems like a lot to endure and it was. But God is faithful. Keep reading.

You may remember from earlier chapters my plight with breast cancer. Thank God for the field of medicine and the hope that it offers. In 2013, God and I battled this Goliath (the giant in my life) called breast cancer and together we won big. I was placed on a medication as part of my post-cancer treatment regimen. This particular medication has been created with great benefits which include decreasing the risk of cancer rearing its ugly head in the breast areas again. But like most medications, there are side effects associated with the use of it. The pharmaceutical information for the medication is clear, suggesting the possibility of birth defects on an unborn child if conception was to occur. And the recommendation for its use requires taking it for ten years to achieve maximum effectiveness. This was a hard pill to swallow for someone hoping to one day conceive. But this minor task could not shake my faith, for God is a God of impossibilities. He's the one who destined that Isaac be born to Abraham and Sarah who were well beyond childbearing age. "So Sarah laughed to herself as she thought, "After I am worn out and my lord (Abraham) is old, will I now have this pleasure?" Then the Lord said to Abraham, "Why did Sarah laugh and say, 'Will I really have a child, now that I am old.' Is anything too hard for the Lord?" (Genesis 18:12-14 NIV) Here is an excerpt from *Unbelief*:

> Sarah laughed, Abraham did too—
> was it their unbelief that made them laugh at You?
> Had they not heard of all You had done,
> or perhaps their minds thought it just could not be overcome?

My faith soared to level five thousand as I envisioned myself as a modern-day Sarah. I looked forward to what was ahead, but my heart still needed to find peace regarding the two unborn children of my past. During the summer of 2014, I joined a Bible study that was tailored to the post-abortive woman and the weight of grief, pain, and shame that many post-abortive women carry. This was an intense ten-week study designed to address every aspect of this unfortunate experience. I suddenly was faced with remembering the *Encounters That Cost* me so much. I had to also come to terms with the emotions that had been swept away during that time. Week by week, my gracious faith-filled facilitators peeled back the layers of pain that held me hostage. I shed so many tears. They covered me and the other bible study participants with love and prayer as me moved through this faith-filled process. Words cannot describe the value of the information received and the relationships built during this pivotal time.

*God's Word is truth and His credibility
has been proven over and over again.*

One of the most extraordinary experiences of this study was a memorial service held for the unborn children. Although our babies found their home with God long ago, as their mothers, we wanted to offer those angels back to Him. This may all sound a bit strange. Trust me, I understand. It was initially a very disturbing thought and almost became the deal breaker for me completing the study. But as the weeks passed and I began to process it, pray about it, and study on God's forgiveness, my feelings began to change. For the first time in my life, I recognized and accepted that I had indeed been a mother (tears are falling as I write). My time with those angels was too short, but my love for them has been lasting. During the memorial, it gave me tremendous joy to name my children Christian and Christiane.¹ Their names represent being Christ-like. I needed to proclaim who they were. I smile as I think about them sitting on God's lap, playing with the other angels. Here's another excerpt from *Encounters That Cost*:

> I stand on God's Word because His promises are true
> He reassures me every day, though you've made mistakes,
> I'm still proud of you
> Your actions did not catch me off guard,
> so I made provisions early on because I knew
> the journey ahead would be hard
> I know the thoughts and plans I have for you
> Grace and mercy will always be there to carry you through
> Hold your head up, release the shame
> Accept my forgiveness and let me wash away that lingering pain
> For my love covers a multitude of sin

Happiness became mine when I released ALL to God (without shame or condemnation) laying every care I had at His feet. As I look back over the pages of my life, I see God's love and His hand of grace and mercy that has carried me. You have heard me reference standing on God's Word throughout this book. That is because God's Word is truth and His credibility has been proven over and over again. He is all wise and I have come to know and trust Him as being just that. Has the journey been easy? Absolutely not. I will admit I still have moments when I wonder *what if* and *how come*. But I have accepted God's complete will for myself and I've gotten in step with Him. He's rapidly moving things along in my life. At times, I struggle to keep up. But I'm determined to go all the way with God. I look to Him and every day I trust Him more and more. I awake with a grateful heart daily, realizing that because of Him happiness is not just mine for the asking, but happiness is mine for all times.

Once again my loving Father has strategically orchestrated the events in my life. He has thrusted me forward in purpose. I am ARMed, doing what He has created me and only me to do, and I am ecstatic about it. The joy of being Christian and Christiane's mother has removed the power of pain, the stench of shame, and the unwarranted place of unforgiveness. Authenticity with God has finally freed me, and it will free you. I am at peace. Peace has opened the door for real lasting happiness and I am walking through it. Unmask your authenticity and walk in it with me.

CHAPTER SEVEN
Becoming Authentic Evermore

The term *bae* has been used for more years than I can remember. It is thought to be a term of endearment spoken between men and women. For this select group, there is no difference in what bae means. But tone of voice may suggest a difference in how it may be interpreted. Women may softly cry out "Bae" when we need our man to change the light bulb that has burned out in the bathroom. It's a gentle cry for help to our knight in shining armor. And men may firmly call out "Bae" when they need their lady to help them locate a matching pair of socks, demonstrating an unmatched need for their queen. Despite the scenario, everyone knows what bae means.

But *Be Authentic Evermore (BAE)* puts a very different spin on this widely used term. It defines a lifestyle that is consistently real and organic in nature. And who doesn't love things that are organic since they lack nothing in quality? Living an authentic evermore lifestyle gives you the opportunity to exhibit this same level of quality. Your character speaks to your credibility. Your integrity becomes contagious. And your level of moral behavior magnetically draws others to you. Your genuine persona is on parade for all to see as you present the rare, priceless jewel that you are day in and day out.

Truly, truly, I say to you, whoever believes in me will also do the works that I do; and greater works than these will he do, because I am going to the Father (John 14:12 ESV).

The benefits of BAE are lasting because it requires closeness with God that can always be cherished. When we think about someone being ARMed, our suggestion makes us conclude that a degree of power is present. This same conclusion may be made when you ARM yourself for the greatness that God has placed in you. Intimacy with God opens the door for obedience and obedience paves the way for authenticity. As I reflect on the information contained within the pages of this book, I am awed by God and pretty amazed at myself. I had no idea God would use my process of self-discovery to impact the lives of others in such a revelatory way. Once again, I must admit, there were several occasions where I struggled to disclose intimate details of my life. But my obedience and trust in God outweighed the fear that attempted to withhold my authenticity from you. Where God wants to take you after you read through the pages of this book is more important to me than hiding my truth from you.

Choosing to reveal the pure version of yourself to others is an easy choice when you stand on God's promises. He is a great God and He does everything in an outstanding manner. Before Jesus—God, the Son—met His fate on the cross, He assured the disciples that "Truly, truly, I say to you, whoever believes in me will also do the works that I do; and greater works than these will he do, because I am going to the Father" (John 14:12 ESV). I began this book with the statement, "There is greatness in you and it resides in your authenticity," and I have chosen to end it with the same statement. Authenticity and greatness abide in you. See it, tap into it, and live it evermore.

Authenticity Reigns Part 2

Authenticity reigns in this spot where I stand
And when you look at me, you see the entire woman I am
God's creation, His masterpiece, I'm a sight to behold
His character so evident… at least, that's what I'm told,
From cover to cover and beginning to end these words
I've absorbed and God's truth
I have heard
Convinced, to be anything other than who I am would be simply absurd
No need to compare myself to you or you to me
My uniqueness, my story no longer needs to hide in obscurity
I am great in His eyes and my success is held in His hands
I just need to sit back, relax… let Him take the wheel and follow His plan
My Father, the King owns my destiny
And when I follow His lead, He brings out the best in me
From sea to shining sea and shore to shore
My originality on display because I am authentic evermore
I once was lost, but now I'm found
Was blind, but now I too see
I'll wear my authenticity evermore
Because authenticity indeed reigns in me

Authenticity Reigns Declaration

Authenticity reigns in me.

I am assertive and confident in my behavior.

I am unique unlike anyone else. I have purpose and I choose to live purposefully.

I am thoughtful in my thinking and actions.

I am honest and truthful in my character.

I am effectual, creating a positive impact on others.

I am noteworthy, I am beautiful, and I command attention.

I am trustworthy. Your confidence is safe with me.

I am imaginative and creative. I don't live in the box. I think outside of the box.

I am consistent. I maintain good moral principles, and I demonstrate that.

> I once was lost, but now I'm found
> Was blind, but now I see
> I'll wear my authenticity evermore
> Because authenticity indeed reigns in me

Made in the USA
Charleston, SC
29 December 2016